CIRCULAR WALKS
IN CENTRAL WALES

Hazards and Problems
Take Notice, Take Care

The author and the publishers stress that walkers should
be aware of the dangers that may occur on all walks.

- check local weather forecast before walking; do not
  walk up into mist or low clouds

- use local OS maps side by side with walking guides

- wear walking boots and clothing

- do not take any unnecessary risks – conditions can
  change suddenly and can vary from season to season

- take special care when accompanied by children or
  dogs

- when walking on roads, ensure that you are
  conspicuous to traffic from either direction

Circular Walks
in
Central Wales

Stephen Edwards

First published in 1998 by Gwasg Carreg Gwalch,
12 Iard yr Orsaf, Llanrwst, Wales LL26 0EH
☎ (01492) 642031
Printed and published in Wales.

*To my mother,
who gave me my love of books,
and my father,
who gave me my love of walking.*

Contents

Features

LOCATION MAP

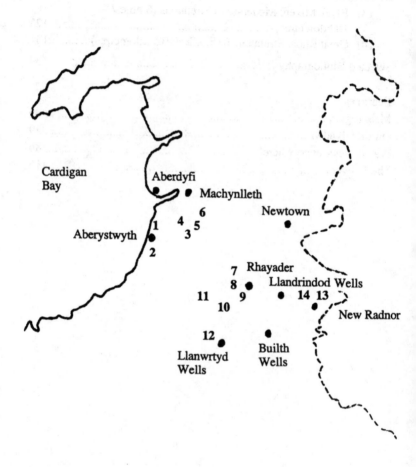

Cardigan
Bay

Aberdyfi
Machynlleth

Newtown

6

1
4 5
Aberystwyth
3

2

7 Rhayader

8 Llandrindod Wells

11 9 14 13

10

New Radnor

12

Llanwrtyd
Wells

Builth
Wells

Introduction

Where is Central Wales?

To most visitors to Wales - and probably to most Welsh people themselves - there are two parts to Wales: northern and southern. South Wales is home to the great population centres - Cardiff, Swansea, Newport, the great valleys of Gwent and Glamorgan - and has been the heartland of Welsh industry for generations. North Wales, on the other hand, boasts smaller towns, and contains popular seaside resorts such as Rhyl, Colwyn Bay, and Llandudno. To the walker, South Wales is home to the Brecon Beacons and associated mountain ranges, and to the Pembrokeshire Coast National Park with its famous long distance footpath, while North Wales is home to the quintessential Welsh walking country - Snowdonia. Indeed, it is often said that over 90% of all leisure walking activity in Wales takes place within five miles of Snowdon itself. Together, it seems, the North and the South make up the nation of Wales.

But do they? There are a whole host of towns - Aberystwyth, Rhayader, Builth Wells, and Newtown among them - that belong neither to the North nor to the South. They belong to a third Wales, Central Wales, a rural heartland that is sparsely populated but bursting with natural beauty. There is little industry here, but many farms. There are no towering peaks here, but many hills. Central Wales has a great deal to offer the walker.

I have walked the length and breadth of Wales, but I have slowly come to the realisation that Central Wales offers more to me as a walker than the North Wales of my birth or the South Wales of my domicile. The greatest peak in the North is, of course, Snowdon, while the finest of the South is Pen y Fan. These are great mountains that offer great walking, and present some of the most spectacular views that one could wish for. But these places offer other views as well that are, perhaps, less desirable to the walker, for it is difficult, if not impossible, to visit these majestic hills without seeing lots and lots of people. It is exhilarating to stand on the roof of Wales, but there is never any feeling of solitude. There is a cafe on the top of Snowdon, and a railway station, and, except in the very worst weather when only a fool would venture up, there are always people. Pen y Fan, on the other hand, has no buildings at its peak, but it always has people. At the feet of these great mountains, among the lay-bys and car parks, there are even more people: ice-cream vans and picnickers and touring couples with fold-up chairs and flasks of tea. This is wilderness country, but there is no feeling of wilderness. There are, though, many tourists and much commercialisation, and somehow, for me, it doesn't quite provide what I really want out of walking.

There are tourists and commercialisation in Central Wales too, of course, but it is on a much smaller scale. Here it is possible to experience a real feeling of wilderness. I have stood on the summit of Pumlumon Fawr, the greatest mountain of Central Wales, on a Bank Holiday Monday in August, and there has been no other human being in sight. I have rambled around the gently rippling reservoirs of the Elan Valley on an Indian summer Sunday and the only evidence of other people has been the reservoirs and walking trails themselves, created by people for people. At last, here in Central Wales, I have found the clear air of archetypal Welsh countryside seemingly free for me to enjoy by myself. It is something of an illusion, of course, for these small islands are too crowded with people for one ever to be truly isolated - there are always farmers at work, anglers crouched by the lakeside trying to out-think the cunning trout, or other walkers after the same experience of the great outdoors as oneself. But still, there are no crowds and no throngs. It is easy to become at peace with oneself and the landscape.

It is the peace of this spectacular landscape that makes Central Wales special. Perhaps it would be hyperbole to describe Central Wales as the jewel in Wales' crown, but a jewel it is all the same. Of all the areas of Wales, it is the least commercialised, and the great throngs of tourists that provide such a welcome boost to the economy of Wales do not yet seem to have discovered its charm. It remains free and unspoilt for us to enjoy.

The History of Central Wales

In order to understand the history of Central Wales, it is necessary always to remember one simple fact: there are not now, nor have there even been, very many people living in Central Wales. Indeed, until the Middle Ages, it is very difficult to find many references to Central Wales in the history books at all. It is almost as if it didn't exist.

It did exist, of course, though a glance at the map today will suggest why Central Wales has but a modest place in the broad picture of Welsh history. For Central Wales is difficult country - the very aspects of Central Wales that make it so attractive to tourists today made it unyielding to our ancestors of long ago. The central massif, from Pumlumon in the west to the Radnor Forest in the east, made this land difficult to farm, and such land, beautiful though it may be, was not conducive to the development of settlements and the emergence of a cradle of civilisation. The lands to the north and south, where the mountain country is more dramatic but more compact in area, and where the soil was more fertile, were more attractive to settlers.

In fact, about twelve thousand years ago, the lands of Central Wales were not so much difficult to live in as well nigh impossible. This was the time of the last great Ice Age, and virtually the whole of what is now Wales, with the exception of a few southerly areas such as the Gower peninsula, were covered with massive ice sheets. However, over the next few thousand years the ice retreated, and human habitation gradually became possible once again throughout the country. This was the time of the Old Stone Age, and the truth is that we know little or nothing about the humans that were around at that time. It is thought that they were most likely to be nomadic in their habits, looking for food and shelter as and when they could, moving on when necessary. Indeed, it is possible that they first reached Wales as a result of their nomadic tendencies, as at that time Britain was not an island. The landbridge to Europe would survive until at least 6000 BC, when the level of the sea started to rise as the retreating ice sheets melted.

Eventually, the Old Stone Age gave way to the Middle Stone Age. About seven thousand years ago, however, the most important advance in the history of mankind took place: for the first time, humans started to cultivate the land. Agriculture had arrived, and the consequences for the peoples of the emerging New Stone Age were to be enormous. Since it was now possible to grow your own food, it became possible to plan food production rather than having to wander about looking for it. This made it advantageous, even necessary, to stay in one place for prolonged periods of time. The nomadic life withered, to be replaced by permanent settlements and the emergence of villages. The new stability allowed the development of social structures and hierarchies, and since the food supply was now more or less assured it gave these Neolithic peoples time to develop a culture. Arts and crafts were allowed to flourish. Tools became more sophisticated. The rate of learning and development was starting to accelerate.

Then, about four thousand years ago, a new element entered the scene: the so-called Beaker folk. The Neolithic communities had taken the great step forward of developing agriculture, but they had been handicapped in their development by their ignorance of the ways of metalworking. On the other hand, the Beaker folk, who had migrated from eastern Europe, were the harbingers of the Bronze Age. They had figured out how to make tools - and weapons - from copper and tin, and this gave them a marked superiority. It is by no means clear how the clash of cultures between Neolithic communities and the Beaker folk was played out all those thousands of years ago. What is clear, however, is that the technological superiority of the Beaker folk gave them the upper hand very quickly. The Neolithic Age was over. The Bronze Age had begun.

We know much more about the Bronze Age in Wales. It lasted for about a millennium and a half, and its peoples were probably the first to make their presence really felt in Central Wales. Most Neolithic remains that have been discovered in Wales are to be found in the north and the south of the country, but Bronze Age burial mounds are to be found right across Central Wales as well. This tells us something about the social structure of these Bronze Age peoples, for the long barrows which were used as cemeteries by the settled Neolithic peoples, and which were probably used as communal burial grounds by villages, were superseded by smaller burial mounds containing usually the remains of only one or two bodies. This suggested that community leaders were afforded important rituals of burial, in turn suggesting that the hierarchy of the social structure was better established. It is also thought that the climate of the area of Central Wales, including the higher ground which had hitherto been somewhat inhospitable, was now easier to endure. Mankind had really arrived in Central Wales, and although it was never to expand to a large population it was never to leave.

The next major upheaval was to occur around two and a half thousand years ago. At the time when Siddhartha Gautama, the man later to be known as the Buddha, was starting to spread his teachings in northern India, and a full five centuries before the birth of Christ, a new wave of peoples arrived in Britain carrying a new technology with them: iron. Iron is a harder metal than bronze. Iron tools are likely to be more efficient than bronze tools - and a skilfully wielded iron sword might well be expected to defeat a bronze sword. The people bringing this new technology were the Celts, and they heralded the end of the Bronze Age and the start of the Iron Age in Britain.

Unfortunately for the indigenous Bronze Age communities, the Celts came not as peaceful teachers of this new technology but as warriors, and their invasion was so successful that it was they who would later become characterised at the archetypal Ancient Britons. The Celts, however, were as prone to fighting amongst themselves as they were to subjugating their predecessors, and it seems likely that there was a prolonged period of cut and thrust before the tribal organisation, that historians recognise today, became established.

It has been pointed out by more than one historian that it is all too easy to get the impression from history books that Wales, indeed Britain, was carved up neatly between the various tribes rather like modern nation-states are neatly divided up on the map today. This was almost certainly not the case. For one thing, the population of the country was far, far less than it is today, and there would have been considerable distance between the various communities. For another, an awful lot of the country, particularly in Wales, would have been pretty much uninhabitable. The mountains of Snowdonia, for example, may have made a great bolt-hole in times of trouble, but the gentler, more fertile valleys would have been a much better place to live if you had the choice. Rather, the areas that became the four main tribal homelands of Wales would have been ill-defined at the borders, and would have been fairly sparsely populated at the best of times. Nevertheless, it is interesting to consider the distribution of these tribal homelands, particularly when you are trying to unravel the history of Central Wales.

In the south, the Silures occupied south-east Wales, in areas that would now be considered to be part of Gwent and much of Glamorgan, while the Demetae occupied south-west Wales, in an area centring on Carmarthen. In the north, the Ordovices occupied north-west Wales, including lands to the south and east of Snowdonia, while the Deceangli occupied north-east Wales, particularly the northern coastal areas. So what of Central Wales? Did any of these warlike Celts consider Central Wales to be worthy of their attention?

The answer to this question is not straightforward. It is, indeed, necessary to weigh up two opposing ideas. On the one hand, it is quite clear that the centres of the Celtic tribal homelands were pretty much based in the extreme north and extreme south of the country. On the other hand, however, it is also clear that the Celts did occupy many area of Central Wales. In Aberystwyth, for example, the hillfort at Pendinas (which will be seen in Walk 1 in this book) was constructed in about 300 BC. Yet it is undeniable that the most impressive concentrations of pre-Roman Celtic remains are not to be found in Central Wales. Then, as before and as now, it was sparsely populated.

Although it is the Celts that are widely viewed as the progenitors of the modern population of Wales, it is interesting to note that they held unchallenged supremacy in Wales for only about 500 years, which is considerably less than the periods of the Bronze Age (something over 1,000 years), the New Stone Age (roughly 3,500 years), or the Middle (roughly 1,000 years) or Old (well over 6,000 years) Stone Ages. Nevertheless, it is possible to chart the acceleration of human progress over this time, and the Celts had developed an advanced civilisation, rich in art and culture, that was about as far removed from the Old Stone Age as could be imagined. The Celts, however, were in for a bit of a shock.

After an abortive first stab into the island of Britain, the Romans

14

finally decided to move in for good in the first century AD. It was not an easy process. The Celts, after all, were a warrior race, but they were ill-disciplined and prone to factionalism. The Romans, on the other hand, were supremely well organised, and possessed an army well-versed in the arts of coming, seeing and conquering. Within a few years it was all over bar the shouting. A garrison at Chester was the base for the subjugation of North Wales, and a garrison at Caerleon served the same purpose for the south. Central Wales, meanwhile, was approached from Wroxeter, and despite the relative ease with which Central Wales must have fallen, it is interesting to note that the Romans took Central Wales seriously enough to build a number of forts to consolidate and maintain their control over the area (a number of these will be visited on the walks in this book). The Romans were, in some ways, brutal imperialists - the infamous massacre of the Druids on Anglesey was enough to seal their reputation in this respect - but they were also inclusive. The supremacy of the Celts was over, but the more pliable elements of the Celtic tribes were to be integrated into the Roman Empire as citizens, rather than as a wholly subjugated slave race. Insofar as the Celtic culture had ever been "pure", it would be pure no longer, but it would not die out. For the Romano-Celtic era had begun, and if the Celts would never again be the undiluted masters in their own home, they would at least survive, incorporating Celtic and Roman elements into a new emerging culture that would last for hundreds of years.

Eventually, as the Roman Empire slowly crumbled, and as they withdrew from Wales towards the end of the fourth century AD, the Celts once again found themselves in charge of their own destiny. Wales, and Britain, once again fell apart into a patchwork of fiefdoms, constantly quarrelling and bickering and fighting. By this time the Celts had been Christianized, though it has to be said that the Christian message of peace seemed to have little effect on the internecine warfare. There was soon to be a new external threat to the Celts, however: the Saxons.

It is a widely accepted idea in Welsh history that the Saxons and Angles were the archetypal bad guys, who quietly stole what is now called England and made the Celts' lives a misery. Indeed, much of

Arthurian legend derives from this era and this tradition. It is true, of course, that the Celtic tribes occupying England may have thought much along these lines; after all, invasion is never terribly popular. But for Wales itself - or for what was to become Wales - the idea is perhaps a trifle overblown. For the tribes of Wales, the Saxons represented a new source of potential allies to be used in fights with neighbouring kingdoms or princedoms. Indeed, the history of Wales from the Saxon invasion to the Norman invasion is not so much one of Saxon infamy, but of Celtic infamy against Celt, with the Saxons playing a walk-on role in alliance with one side or the other. This is not to say that the Saxons never caused any problems for the Welsh. For the eastern Welsh, in particular, they could be an out and out pain in the neck. But it would be false to consider the Saxons as entirely at fault. The Celts were, in some respects, their own worst enemies. Paradoxically, although this era is known elsewhere as the Dark Ages, within Wales it is often referred to as the Golden Age, for although life was dominated for long periods by bouts of pointless warfare against one's neighbours it was also characterised, in cultural terms, by the emergence of great traditions of story-telling and poetry. The tales of the Mabinogion, and the poetry of Taliesin, which are thought to originate from roughly this period, represent some of the earliest and finest examples of literature in any modern European language.

If the Saxons are popularly thought to be the villains of Welsh history, however, it is the Normans who really deserve the accolade. More than anyone else, it was the Normans who ended any idea of genuine self-rule for the Welsh right up to the modern era. After the invasion of 1066 the Saxons were well and truly scuppered, and the Celts of Wales yet again had to contemplate the prospect of a more powerful invading force knocking at the door. They weren't left to think about it for long. The Normans forced their way into North Wales via Chester, and into South Wales via Caerleon, just as the Romans had done. For Central Wales, however, the threat this time came from Shrewsbury and Hereford, which had evolved into major centres just across Offa's Dyke. Before long, Wales was littered with Norman castles and was well and truly in Norman hands. Life would never be the same again.

Over the next few centuries, in the period often referred to as the Medieval Era, the story of Wales was one of periodic re-organisation of political power amongst the Welsh princes and Norman lordships, and of occasional full-blown rebellion against the English crown. Interestingly, and for the first time, Central Wales took centre stage in a number of critical events. Of particular note was the rebellion against Edward I of Llywelyn ap Gruffudd in 1282. Widely regarded as the last genuine Prince of Wales by line of blood, Llywelyn led a coalition of Welsh forces against Edward which was ultimately to end in failure. Llywelyn met his end at the hands of the Normans (who by now could be more or less considered as English), and was murdered at Cilmeri (just west of Builth Wells) where today a monument marks the event. Dafydd, his brother, took over leadership of the doomed rebellion but he was captured by Edward before being hanged, drawn and quartered at Shrewsbury the following year. Indeed, he is reputed to have been the first man ever to have subjected to this hideous punishment.

Even more notable, though, was the role of Central Wales in the later rebellion of Owain Glyndŵr in the early fifteenth century. Owain was an unlikely hero, though he ultimately became responsible for the last fully-fledged armed rebellion against the crown before his defeat by Henry IV, and in the process he entered the pantheon of Welsh heroes as probably the greatest Welshman who ever lived (much more information on Owain is given in Walk 4, which passes close to the scene of one of his greatest battles).

For most of the past five centuries, however, Central Wales has reverted back to what it has been for most of its history: a beautiful, though sometimes inhospitable, thinly populated area sandwiched between the historically more eventful north and south of Wales. Its towns are small, its villages sleepy. Yet even quiet, picturesque Central Wales has its history which is there, in the landscape, for the walker to seek it out. Many of the walks within this book are designed to help you do that, and it is one of the unsung glories of Central Wales that the walker can feel the resonance of all the ages amongst some of the most beautiful countryside to be found anywhere in Wales.

Walking in Central Wales

One of the pleasures of being a walker is that you do not actually have to be walking to enjoy your hobby. On dark, miserable winter days, when only the masochistic are out on the mountains getting soaked to the skin, the walker can enjoy poring over maps, planning days out for when the weather improves. As far as Central Wales is concerned, such activity with maps can be a joy and a frustration, for it sometimes seems that the whole area is ripe for walking. There is always one more hill to climb, or one more mountain lake or tarn that you want to see.

The maps do not lie, for most of Central Wales is indeed ripe for walking. Whether it is exploring valleys or climbing hills or mountains, there is no shortage of outdoors experience for the adventurous to enjoy. I am never quite sure if there is such a thing as a "typical" Central Wales walk - every time I think I've got Central Wales figured out a new walk comes along to shatter my illusions - but it is certainly true that Central Wales is characterised by the so-called Cambrian mountains. From Pumlumon to the west to Radnor Forest to the east, Central Wales has a collection of mountain groups that are each part of this central massif - perhaps the true dividing line between North and South Wales - yet each have their own quirks and characteristics. In selecting the walks for this book, I have tried to highlight the character of each group, and in addition I have tried also to include some of those areas in between that are so rich in history.

In the far west lies Aberystwyth, staring out over Cardigan Bay and the Irish Sea, with its twin hills sandwiching the town between them. Both will be visited, providing easy walks to start the book. Nestling inland from Aberystwyth is the most famous, and perhaps the most splendid, of the Cambrian mountain groups: Pumlumon. I have chosen four walks around rocky, craggy Pumlumon, including Pumlumon Fawr itself, the highest point in Central Wales. Further east lies Rhayader, gateway to the lovely Elan Valley with its sprawling reservoirs and plentiful historic remains. Three walks will guide you around this area, including a visit to the Elan Valley Visitor Centre and its associated nature reserve. South of the Elan Valley lies Llanwrtyd Wells and the mysterious Cwmdeuddwr hills, the very epitome of wilderness. Again, I have chosen three walks here to highlight the wonderful peace and solitude of this empty yet beautiful country. Last, but not least, there is the Radnor Forest, a forest in name only and tucked just inside the border. Here, vast high plateaux command the pretty valleys between, and the unusual may be found in the most unexpected places. Two walks will guide you around this unusual corner of Wales.

I have tried to classify the walks in this book very roughly as easy, moderate or strenuous, simply in an effort to indicate an approximate level of difficulty that is self-explanatory. All the walks are circular, at least in the sense that the start point and end point are the same. For some walks it is possible to give a return route that is different to the outwards route (e.g. walk 3: Pumlumon Fawr). For others, it is impossible to do so without making the walk unattractively long or difficult. For each walk, very detailed instructions are given. However, I would encourage walkers to regard these walks merely as a starting point for an appreciation of Central Wales. When one is experienced enough and confident enough, the very best walks are those that you have planned yourself. In fact, even for some of the walks contained within this book, the more adventurous may wish to construct their own mountain adventures based on the information given, and in some cases, two shorter walks may be combined to form a single long walk (a few suggestions are included). Alternatively, many of the walks here follow routes close to some interesting centres, such as Aberystwyth or Rhayader, and a long summer's day out can be planned incorporating the walk into a more general exploration of these places. The choice is entirely yours.

The routes in this book include walking of two types. The first is following rights-of-way, and the second is across open countryside. The issue of rights-of-way, and of the right to roam, are often controversial. Organisations such as the Ramblers one the one hand, and the Country Landowners Association on the other, are frequently at loggerheads over the idea of walkers trampling across countryside. It is not my intention, here, to lead walkers into controversy. The vast majority of the routes followed in this book follow defined rights-of-way as shown on Ordinance Survey maps. Most are very clearly defined footpaths or bridleways, and all have been thoroughly test-walked to ensure that the routes do not lead the walker into trespassing or into areas where walkers may be likely to be irritating to farmers or landowners. Occasionally, however, it is inevitable that walking to some of the more isolated peaks will involve crossing open countryside away from clearly defined bridleways. Again, in all cases the routes have been thoroughly test-walked, and all the directions given have been specifically designed to avoid giving offence to landowners. Whenever you follow the directions in this book off established footpaths and bridleways you will only be entering genuinely wild land, and wherever possible I have directed walkers onto paths which may not appear on Ordinance Survey maps, but which have been evident on the ground, and used by walkers, for many, many years. It is still, though, an obligation of the walker to remember that all land is owned by somebody somewhere, and all walkers should keep to the country code at all times.

Safety

The walks in this book are not designed for the training of SAS commandos or Royal Marines - they are designed to provide enjoyment for people who, like me, are of merely average fitness and happen to gain pleasure from the great outdoors. In walking terms, there is nothing inherently unsafe about the routes described. There are no tricky rock scrambles to attempt, and there are no quaking bogs into which unwary ramblers may sink to their doom. Perhaps the greatest hazard you would be likely to encounter would be the danger of wet feet! And yet, even the very simplest walk can lead the careless into unnecessarily difficult situations if the most basic precautions are not taken.

I found this out the hard way. Several summers ago, my partner and I decided to take advantage of some fine weather to undertake a simple ramble in the Brecon Beacons National Park. It was sunny and warm, there wasn't a cloud in the sky, and our walk was a straightforward low-level affair that would never take us more than a kilometre from a road. Nothing, it seemed, could go wrong, and with drinking water, sun cream, and a map, we ventured forth. Crucially, we didn't take a compass - a major mistake. After an enjoyable walk we were barely a kilometre from our car when suddenly, out of a cloudless sky, thick mist started to roll in. Within minutes, visibility was down to a few metres and the temperature was starting to drop. We did not have the warm clothing to endure a night out in the country, and without a compass the maze of sheeptracks around us provided total confusion as to the direction we should take. The wisdom of all the warnings in the walking manuals, about how difficult it is to walk a straight line without a compass, quickly became evident. We were in a sticky situation.

Fortunately, though, the situation was not entirely hopeless. We had a map, and the country we were in was contoured, and it was possible to use the direction of the contours to estimate the direction back to the car. As it happened, we emerged out of the mist and back at the road only metres away from where we had parked, but we had been lucky. The failure to carry a compass had been an incredibly stupid thing to do, for this simple apparatus would have enabled us to walk straight back to the car without any difficulty at all. As it was, a really simple stroll had needlessly turned into a nerve-jangling test of map-reading skill. The lesson had been well and truly learnt.

Since this experience I have thought long and hard about walking safety. In truth, country walking is a safe pursuit - you are more likely to come to harm crossing a main road to buy a newspaper. Yet there are some very simple and very basic precautions that every walker should take to ensure that their walk is a pleasure and not a potential hazard, and there are two main considerations is this respect: navigation and weather.

As far as navigation is concerned, the main question that every walker should always have lurking in the back of his or her mind is: what would I do if visibility was suddenly cut down to zero? A fair proportion of the walking described in this book follows well-defined paths, making navigation in zero visibility quite straightforward. However, some of it crosses open moorland and this, of course, is where skill with map and compass comes in. Fortunately, using a map and compass for navigation is a bit like riding a bike - before you have acquired the skill it looks impossibly difficult, yet once you have tried it a few times it dawns on you that it is a very easy thing to do. I would recommend the use of the relevant 1:25 000 scale Ordinance Survey maps (the 1:50 000 are adequate for most purposes, but lack the fine detail of the 1:25 000 maps, such as field boundaries, which can be very useful), and a decent compass can be bought cheaply from any outdoors shop (Silva compasses, with a rotating dial and a clear plastic base containing an arrow, are probably the most common and are perfectly adequate). Thus equipped, you are set to navigate your way across any walkable terrain.

Perhaps the simplest operation with map and compass is the orientation of the map to the terrain. The compass needle points to magnetic north, and since magnetic north more or less corresponds with the top of the map it is easy to match map with landscape (actually the top of the map corresponds with grid north rather than magnetic north, but over the distances we are covering in this book the difference is so small as to be relatively unimportant). A slightly more sophisticated operation with map and compass is that of taking a bearing. You will notice that the rotating circular compass dial is divided into 360 degrees. North is zero degrees, east is 90 degrees, south is 180 degrees, and so on. Suppose you are stuck in mist, but you know that you need to walk due east to get to a road. You know that due east is 90 degrees, so rotate the dial of the compass until the 90 degree indicator is aligned with the main arrow on the plastic base. Then, slowly pirouette around until the red tip of the compass needle is nestling snugly within the two white lines inside the compass barrel. Once the red needle and the two white lines are neatly lined up, the arrow on the compass base is pointing in the direction that you need to walk (i.e. due east). Simple!

Even using a compass in this way, in thick mist it is difficult to walk accurately in a straight line for any appreciable distance. There may be rocks or awkward tussocks in the way, and there is a tendency for the walker to drift slightly from the intended path. For this reason, it is difficult to walk for any distance to reach a specific point, such as a standing stone or a cairn, because this tendency to drift means you may very easily miss your landmark. Rather than heading for a specific point, therefore, it is better to head for a rather wider target, such as a road, so that even if you do drift somewhat to the right or the left (and you will!) you will still hit the road reasonably close to the place where you intended. It is easy to miss a standing stone situated one kilometre from your starting point, but it is very difficult to miss a road without going hopelessly in the wrong direction - and the compass will prevent you doing that.

Appended to every walk I have given some notes on safety, mostly pertaining to what you should do if suddenly stranded in mist and having to rely on map and compass for navigation. If you are on a clear path, the easiest thing to do is to retrace your steps. However, on open moorland the easiest thing to do usually is to head for the nearest road - you may end up with sore feet having walked rather further than you had originally intended, but at least you will have the security of knowing exactly where you are and exactly where you are going, and if absolutely necessary it may be possible to hitch a lift, reach a telephone, or knock on the door of a farm.

Armed with these simple techniques, even the novice walker can stride out with the confidence that the map and compass provide a safety net should the mist roll in. The great dread of every walker, particularly when on open moorland, is that they should suddenly discover that they are lost. However, this is an unnecessary worry. If you keep checking your map at intervals, you will always know more or less where you are. If the mist suddenly descends when you haven't checked your map for a while, there is no need to panic. After all, walking is a fairly slow activity, and you can only have walked so far from your last known position. You can never be *really* lost! Even if you only know your position to within a kilometre or so (the distance of a grid square on an Ordinance Survey map) it is virtually always possible to decide on a bearing that will bring you to a road or river or other wide, obvious landmark.

The second main safety concern is regarding the weather. In essence, this means staying warm and dry. No matter what the weather is like (or what the weather forecast suggests) I always carry waterproofs, warm clothing (even in August the nights can be nippy), drinking water and spare food. I also carry a safety bag - a simple, cheap brightly covered plastic bag (available from any outdoors shop) that you can climb inside to stay dry and visible should you get stuck for any reason. The key question to ask here is: what would I do if I broke an ankle and couldn't continue walking? Clearly, the priority would be to ensure that the casualty is warm and dry enough to survive comfortably until help arrives. The ideal size for a walking party is usually regarded as a minimum of four people, so that one person can stay with the casualty and two can walk on to summon help. If the walking party is smaller than this, it is sensible to let someone know where you are walking, your route, and your expected time of return, so that if the walkers do not return there is someone who knows that something is amiss and can raise the alarm. It should also be regarded as essential to carry a whistle. Even if help is summoned, it is necessary for the rescuers to find the casualty, and the international distress signal (six blasts on the whistle, followed by a minute's pause, followed by another six blasts, and so on) is an invaluable aid (the reply to the signal is the same only with three blasts on the whistle).

Fortunately, however, although accidents can happen to the best of us, it is fairly unlikely that most careful walkers will require such assistance. It is, of course, important to be prepared for the worst, but most consideration of the weather by the walker consists of enjoying the walk in comfort (i.e. not being cold and wet) and applying a little common sense as to whether the day's weather forecast is reasonable enough to start the walk in the first place. Since a great deal of the pleasure that I derive from walking has its source in the fabulous views that can be enjoyed in our hills and valleys, I have never really seen the point of starting a walk in pouring rain or thick mist. Although winter walking has its own charms, if there is enough snow and frost around to make the going treacherous at the foot of a mountain, the conditions are unlikely to be better at the summit. With the right equipment, it is possible to undertake any of the walks in this book in virtually any weather conditions. But it is as well to remember that the worse the weather, the more likely you are to have an accident, and should a rescue team have to be sent for it is not only your own life that you are risking.

There is, however, one type of weather condition in which walks should not be attempted under any circumstances. If thunder and lightning are expected, it is foolhardy to set out on a route that will inevitably at some point mean you are the highest and most exposed potential lightning conductor on the landscape. Unfortunately, however, thunder storms are most common in summer - the very time when walking is most enjoyable - and are not always predictable. It is, therefore, possible for even the most careful walker to be caught out in this way, and all walkers should be ready to take action if lightning threatens. The best strategy for the walker in this case is clear - avoid becoming a lightning conductor - but the best way to do this is not always obvious and will depend very much upon the terrain being walked. The primary goal is to avoid dangerous areas. Ridges, crests and summits are definitely not the places to be, as you are not only likely to be the tallest object in your immediate surroundings but very high up as well. If you are caught out in such places, the first thing to do is to move away quickly to less exposed and preferably lower ground. It is, of course, necessary to take care doing this; it is one thing to escape lightning, but it is another thing to do this by twisting your ankle, breaking your leg, or falling down a hundred foot sheer drop. The best places to head for are places where you will not be so exposed. Valleys, caves and dense forestry will all provide protection. In expansive flat areas, depressions in the ground are the best bet. Avoid, however, cracks in rocks, very small caves, and either single trees or small groups of them, as these can all attract lightning strikes. If getting to a safe area quickly is not on the cards, there are still some measures that you can take to protect yourself. First, remove metal objects that you may be carrying. These are unlikely to play a major role in attracting lightning - you are much more likely to do that yourself - but should lightning strike then metal objects can heat up incredibly quickly and give severe burns. Next, retrieve from your pack some flat, non-conducting object - a foam mat of the type used by backpackers is perfect for this, although a simple safety bag (which you really ought to be carrying anyway) should also do the trick. Lay this on the ground, then crouch down low on your mat or bag. The key here is to avoid contact with the ground and to keep low. Crouched down, you are less likely to attract a lightning strike, and even if a strike should occur in your vicinity the insulating mat will protect you from the currents flowing around you through the ground.

As the new millennium approaches, complete with its high-tech wizardry, it is worth mentioning two recent items that may provide walkers with an additional safety tool. In any walking magazine, now, it is possible to see advertisements for hand-held GPS units - electronic gizmos that utilise information from orbital satellites to provide a readout of your precise current location, and they can also act as a guidance system. These are undeniably nifty gadgets, though I do not use one and I consider them to be a somewhat expensive luxury. They do not do anything that a properly used map and compass won't do, though my main reservation is that compasses do not need batteries and do not pack up if you accidentally drop them in a stream. Another device that is perhaps more likely to be useful in emergency situations is a mobile phone. However, two words of warning concerning their use: first, it cannot be guaranteed that they will work out in the middle of nowhere; second, use them only in cases of dire emergency. Police or mountain rescue services are unlikely to be impressed if you ring them up to ask for directions off a hill you have just climbed, or to tell them it's just started raining and you don't have a waterproof with you.

More than anything else, safety while walking is a matter of common sense, and it is quite possible to kit yourself out for a smashing day's walk in perfect safety without breaking the bank. I must confess that I am not hugely impressed with the ever more high-tech - and expensive - equipment that one sees advertised in walking magazines. It seems to me that a lot of that stuff is more suited to an expedition in the Antarctic rather than a pleasant day out among the hills of Central Wales. Nevertheless, there is one piece of kit that I do not skimp on, and that is walking boots. Nothing spoils an otherwise cracking walk like hurting feet, yet with decent boots there is no reason in the world why your feet should hurt - the days of hob-nailed clodhoppers are long gone. Everybody has different feet with different characteristics, and the best advice I can give is to go to a small but reputable outdoors shop, staffed by people who are knowledgeable and experienced walkers, and seek their advice. Good shops will stock boots in half sizes and with various width fittings. And don't be shy or feel daft about this - I am one of those unfortunate people with awkwardly-sized feet, and as a consequence I wear ladies boots. I felt a bit silly buying them, but my word it was worth it. After all, once you leave the shop who will ever know?

Country Code

All walkers must keep to the country code at all times:
Enjoy the countryside and respect its life and work
Guard against all risk of fire
Fasten all gates
Keep your dogs under close control
Keep to the public paths across farmland
Use gates and stiles to cross fences, hedges and walls
Leave livestock, crops and machinery alone
Take your litter home
Help to keep all water clean
Protect wildlife, plants and trees
Take special care on country roads
Make no unnecessary noise

Welsh Place Names

Having lived in both Wales and England, it has often stuck me that Welsh language place names are much more expressive of the topography of the area than English place names. This is, of course, partly an illusion. Many English place names were originally highly expressive of their locality but reflect the use of language that is no longer colloquial, and many names have, in any case, changed much over time. Still, it is undeniably true that Welsh place names are highly evocative of place, though this can lead to some interesting cultural phenomena. It is said, for example, that Eskimos have about thirty different names for snow, which is hardly surprising when they are surrounded by the stuff all the time. The same sort of thing happens in Welsh, only this time for geographical features like valleys, hills, moors and rivers. For example, both *cwm* and *dyffryn* mean "valley", though typically the term *cwm* is applied to a deep, large, spectacular valley (of the type that is usually associated with the great valleys of South Wales, such as *Cwm Rhondda*), whereas the term *dyffryn* is more usually applied to shallower, more rambling, and less dramatic valleys (such as the Vales of Glamorgan and Clwyd). You will, no doubt, be able to identify further examples of this from your own experiences of walking in Wales. A second phenomenon is that since the names of Welsh paces are often very simple (e.g. *Tŷ Coch*, literally Red House), it is very often found that the same place names crop up again and again, occasionally in disconcertingly close proximity. It is, perhaps, worth remembering that while a distance of ten or twenty miles might now be trivial to someone in a motor car, in days of old when these names were first coined these were often very significant distances indeed.

The following is a list of Welsh place name terms that you are likely to come across while walking the routes given in this book:

Aber – Mouth of a river	*Dau* – Two
Afon – River	*Deri* – Oak
Allt – Hill, wood	*Dinas* – City, hillfort
Bach – Little	*Dôl* – Meadow
Bryn – Hill	*Du* – Black
Bwlch – Pass	*Dŵr* – Water
Caer – Castle, fort	*Dyffryn* – Valley
Canol – Centre, middle	*Efail* – Smithy
Capel – Chapel	*Eglwys* – Church
Carn – Cairn	*Ffordd* – Road
Carreg – Rock, stone	*Ffos* – Ditch, dyke
Castell – Castle	*Ffynnon* – Well, spring
Clawdd – Dyke	*Gelli* – Grove
Coch – Red	*Glan* – Riverbank
Coed – Wood	*Gwastad* – Flat, level
Cors – Bog	*Gwaun* – Moor
Craig – Crag, rock	*Gwyn* – White
Crib – Ridge	*Gwynt* – Wind
Croes – Cross	*Hafod* – Summer dwelling
Cwm – Valley	*Hen* – Old

Hendre – Winter dwelling
Isaf – Lower
Llan – Church
Llannerch – Clearing, glade
Llyn – Lake
Llwybr – Path
Llwyd – Grey
Maen – Stone
Maes – Field
Mawr – Big, great
Melin – Mill
Melyn – Yellow, blond
Moel – Hill
Morfa – Marsh
Mynach – Monk
Mynydd – Mountain
Nant – Stream

Newydd – New
Nos – Night
Ogof – Cave
Parc – Park
Pen – Top, head, end
Pentre – Village
Plas – Hall, large house
Pont – Bridge
Pwll – Pool, pit
Rhiw – Hill
Rhos – Moor
Rhyd – Ford
Sych – Dry
Tref – Town
Tŷ – House
Uchaf – Upper
Y, Yr – The
Yn – In

Pronunciation of Welsh is both easy and difficult. It is generally easier than English because Welsh is mostly phonetical, but it is difficult for an English tongue because many of the sounds are not found in English. Consonants such as *c* and *g* are always pronounced hard (as in cake or gate), though vowels (which include *w* and *y* in Welsh) may be pronounced long or short. The letter *f* on its own is always pronounced as a *v* in English, whereas a double *ff* is pronounced as an *f* in English. The really difficult ones, though, are *ch*, *dd* and *ll*.

The letter *ch* (the two letters in the Roman script count as a single letter in the Welsh alphabet, which is quite different to the English alphabet) is usually described in books as being pronounced as the *ch* in the Scottish *loch*. However, since most English people seem to pronounce *loch* as "lock", this is probably not very helpful. The *ch* sound resembles the sound you make when you clear your throat. Try saying "yuck" as if you are trying to clear mucous out of your throat and are about to spit.

The letter *dd* is much easier. The sound of this is exactly the same as the *th* in the English word *they*. The letter *ll* is harder, though, and I have not seen this sound in any non-Celtic language. The nearest most non-Welsh people can get at first is to place the tongue on the roof of the mouth as if you are about to say the letter *l*, then breathe out heavily. Failing this, pronouncing *ll* as *thl* is better than nothing, although it may make you sound as if you have a lisp!

Useful Information

Tourist Information Centres (* open all year)

Aberystwyth*	Tel 01970 - 612125
Builth Wells*	Tel 01982 - 553307
Llanidloes*	Tel 01686 - 412605
Llandrindod Wells*	Tel 01597 - 822600
Llanwrtyd Wells	Tel 01591 - 610666
Newtown*	Tel 01686 - 625580
Rhayader*	Tel 01597 - 810591

Other Useful Numbers

Elan Valley Visitor Centre	Tel 01597 - 810880
Glyndŵr Way Project Officer	Tel 01547 - 529179
Nant yr Arian Forest Centre	Tel 01970 - 890694
Offa's Dyke Association	Tel 01547 - 528753
Public Transport Enquiry Lines	
Ceredigion	Tel 01545 - 572504
Powys	Tel 01597 - 826643
Rambler's Association (Welsh Office)	Tel 01978 - 855148
Vale of Rheidol Railway	Tel 01970 - 625819
Weathercall	Tel 0891 - 500414
Ystumtuen Youth Hostel (Aberystwyth)	Tel 01970 - 890693

Other Walks

There are a number of long distance routes to be found in the area or passing through it. The following are a selection of the most popular:

Offa's Dyke Path

This official national trail runs from Prestatyn on the north coast to Chepstow on the south coast. It is 168 miles (270 km) long, and for most of its length it follows the line of the dyke itself. Numerous guides to this path have been published.

Glyndŵr Way

This horseshoe shaped route runs from Welshpool to Machynlleth, then back to Knighton. It is 128 miles (206 km) long, and is designed to pass as many sites relevant to the history of Owain Glyndŵr as possible. An application for national trail status is currently being considered. A guide to this path has been published by Constable.

Wye Valley Walk

This trail runs from Chepstow to Rhayader, via Monmouth, Hereford and Builth Wells. It is 107 miles (172 km) long, and follows the course of the River Wye. At least two guides to this route are currently available, one of which may be obtained from Powys County Council.

Cambrian Way

A gruelling 274 mile (440 km) route from the north coast at Conwy to the south coast at Cardiff, via Snowdonia and the Brecon Beacons. A guide to this route has been self-published by its founder, Tony Drake, and can be obtained from the Ramblers Association.

Elan Valley Trail

This shorter 5 mile (8 km) trail runs from the Elan Valley Visitor Centre to the Craig Goch Reservoir. A guide to this path is available from the Elan Valley Visitor Centre.

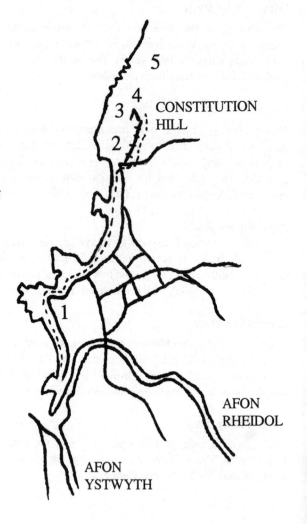

CARDIGAN
BAY

CONSTITUTION
HILL

5

4

3

2

1

AFON
RHEIDOL

AFON
YSTWYTH

Aberystwyth Harbour - Constitution Hill

OS Maps: 1:50 000 Landranger 135 (Aberystwyth); 1:25 000
              Pathfinder 926 (SN 57/58: Aberystwyth).

Start: Aberystwyth Harbour.

Access: Aberystwyth is easily reached via the A44 from the east,
              or the A487 from the north or south. Aberystwyth
              Harbour is signposted from the town centre.

Parking: Parking is available at the harbour itself. Alternatively,
              if parking is difficult during the peak tourist season, it is
              possible to park at almost any point along the sea front
              (in which case your parking place can be treated as a
              different start point, as everywhere you could
              conceivably park along the front forms part of the walk
              anyway).

Grade: Easy - involves about 100m ascent in total. Sea front
              and well defined paths. Walking boots not necessary -
              training shoes would be quite adequate. Note that if you
              decide to walk the Constitution Hill Nature Trail, this
              will roughly double the length of the walk, though it is
              all pretty easy going.

*A simple walk to start the book, giving a flavour of Aberystwyth's
eccentric past and providing wonderful views across Cardigan Bay. A
possible extension is suggested, that includes one of Wales' prettiest
nature trails.*

Points of Interest:

1. Aberystwyth Castle. The first castle at Aberystwyth was built by
Norman invaders in 1110 as part of a chain of castles designed to
subjugate North Wales. This was a straightforward wood and earth
structure that evidently provided much sport for the local population,
who burned it down a number of times before it was finally rebuilt in

stone by Edward I. This was an altogether more substantial structure, defended by thick walls and a moat, which repelled local resistance until it was eventually captured by Owain Glyndŵr in 1404. It served as one of his headquarters' for four years or so, until Henry of Monmouth recaptured it for the Normans with the aid of the "King's Gun", a four and a half ton piece of artillery specially imported from Nottingham for the job. Today, little is left of the castle - though most of one tower remains to remind us of its history. It overlooks the sea front, its positioning allowing it to be supplied by sea while it was in use.

2. Aberystwyth Electric Cliff Railway. Built in 1896, this delightful and eccentric funicular railway runs to the summit of Constitution Hill. It was engineered by George Croydon Marks, who also had a hand in the rebuilding of the Royal Pier (encountered earlier in the walk) and the development of the Vale of Rheidol narrow-gauge railway. The carriages are hauled up the hill using ropes, and originally the power to do so was provided by filling up 1,000 gallon water tanks attached to the front of the descending carriages (thus enabling the attached ascending carriages to make the trip to the top by gravitational power), though of course these days it is all motorised. George Croydon Marks himself was quite a notable local character. He later moved into a political career, becoming an Aberystwyth town councillor before being elected as the Liberal M.P. for Launceton in Cornwall in 1906. He was knighted in 1911, awarded the C.B.E. in 1918, and became Baron Marks of Woolwich in 1929. Reputed to be a friend of Thomas Edison, Marks went on to become a founder director of the E.M.I. record company. A trip on Marks' cliff railway currently costs about £2 (though note that the trains only run from March to October).

3. Constitution Hill. This hill, something over 130m or so above sea level at its highest point, dominates the northern aspect of Aberystwyth, just as Pendinas (visited in walk 2) dominates the southern aspect. For my money, Constitution Hill offers the most spectacular view there is of the town of Aberystwyth and, even better, its sea frontage leading out to the expanse of Cardigan Bay. It also gives the best view of Pendinas away to the north, with its very visible monument and its less visible Iron Age fort. A century or so ago,

34

Constitution Hill was the somewhat unlikely focal point of the Central Wales leisure and tourist industry. The Aberystwyth Electric Cliff Railway (see above) was handy for ferrying tourists up to the summit, at which point the leisure-seeking Victorians and Edwardians were presented with a mind-boggling array of amusements, collectively known as "Luna Park", including a bandstand, a ballroom, a tea-room, a roller-coaster ride, and, of course, the *camera obscura* (see below). These days it is a bit less hectic at the top, though the railway still runs and the *camera obscura* is still open from March to October. Also, in keeping with our greener times, there is a nature trail (see below).

4. Camera Obscura. The principle behind the *camera obscura* - or pin-hole camera - is very simple, and the construction of one is something that every school child should try at some time. In the very best *Blue Peter* style, take a shoe-box or similar, and cut out a panel of a few square inches of so on one side, covering the hole with a sheet of tracing paper. On the opposite side of the shoe box, directly opposite the tracing paper viewing panel, use a pin to make a small hole. Now point this "camera" at some easily recognised object not too far away, and with some to-ing and fro-ing and a bit of jiggling about an inverted image of the object should appear in the tracing paper panel. Needless to say, photographic technology has come on a bit since the *camera obscura* was invented round about the thirteenth century, though the same principle is often utilised today by amateur astronomers who wish to observe the sun without burning their eyes out. It is also true that the *camera obscura* atop Constitution Hill is a bit more sophisticated than the average shoebox model. The room-sized *camera obscura* started to appear in the nineteenth century as a popular amusement, and the original model here had its heyday at the turn of the century - the foundations for this can be seen just a few metres away from the current building. This *camera obscura* had a four inch lens and a mirror to enable tourists the view the surrounding area, though when it was re-built and re-opened in 1985 it had acquired a fourteen inch lens and was now the largest in the world, allowing visitors to view over 1,000 square miles of sea and scenery. The image of the Aberystwyth coastline is reflected off a large mirror in the roof and beamed down to a large viewing screen. The mirror can

be rotated by visitors to vary the scene, and it is quite amazing how clear and sharp the image is from such a primitive device. With a bit of luck you might even be able to see your car!

5. Constitution Hill Nature Trail. I have walked many nature trails in my time (another is featured in Walk 8 in the Elan Valley) but this is one of my favourites, not least for the spectacular views across Cardigan Bay to Bardsey Island and for the opportunity to see a wide variety of sea-birds in action. It was prepared by the joint efforts of the Ceredigion branch of the West Wales Naturalists' Trust, Aberystwyth Town Council, and the Aberystwyth Branch of the National Conservation Corps, and although it would add about two and a half miles or so to your walk it is well worth it. Visitors are strongly recommended to purchase a copy of the guide from the cliff railway terminus at the bottom of the hill or the gift shop at the summit. A full map of the trail is given, along with copious notes as to the fauna and flora you might expect to see. A number of marker posts are laid out along the route, and the trail guide describes what you should be able to see at each point. The guide also gives details of other nature trails in the area.

Walk Directions:

1. From the harbour, set off northish along the sea front. You have a choice of two routes here. The easiest (but less interesting) route is to walk around the sea front using the pavement. However, it is more enjoyable - so long as the tide allows - to walk along the beach. There are numerous sets of steps along the sea front, so if you want to walk along the beach you can still fairly easily nip up to the road to take a better look at some of the more interesting items along the road, including the local War Memorial, Aberystwyth Castle [1], and the Royal Pier.

2. Continue around and along the sea front. If walking along the beach, beware of losing your footing on the rockier parts, which can be very slippery. Eventually you will reach the end of the beach with the lower terminus of the Aberystwyth Electric Cliff Railway [2] on your right. Climb up to the terminus entrance. If you plan to walk the nature trail,

it is a good idea to purchase the guide book from the terminus and follow its directions from here. Alternatively, walk up past the terminus entrance to a footpath on the left. Turn left here, and start the short, sharp haul up to the summit of Constitution Hill [3].

3. You will find that there is a veritable rabbit warren of paths leading up to the summit. It doesn't really matter which paths you use, though note that from time to time some paths may be closed off for restoration work, and also note that even open paths can be quite slippery at times. My preferred route up includes crossing at least two of the bridges over the railway - this allows you to catch your breath while appearing to be taking in the view. Soon the summit buildings come into view, including the upper terminus of the railway, the tea shop, gift shop, and the Camera Obscura [4]. It should also be possible to re-join the Constitution Hill Nature Trail [5] up here.

4. From the summit, the route back to the harbour is essentially a case of re-tracing your steps, though of course there is ample opportunity to stop off on the way for sustenance and refreshment (one of the glories of a sea front walk is that you can form a plan of attack for chips and ice-cream on the way back while you are on the way to your destination).

Facilities:

As a tourist seaside town, Aberystwyth has all the facilities that you are ever likely to need. Indeed, since much of the walk follows the sea front you will encounter no shortage of ice-cream shops, chip shops, and even Indian and Chinese take-aways. There is also a tea-room on the summit of Constitution Hill. The harbour also boasts a Royal National Lifeboat Institution station, which includes a gift shop (in, of course, a very good cause). Note that some facilities may be closed during the winter months.

Safety Notes:

As far a navigation is concerned, safety is not much of an issue for this walk - at worst it follows very easily followed paths. There are, however, two safety points that should be noted. The first is to beware of incoming tides if you decide you walk around the sea front along the beach. This is really a matter of common sense - if the tide is high then it would be better to walk along the pavement, and if the tide is rapidly coming in then take advantage of the numerous steps up to the pavement to avoid getting your feet wet. The second point concerns the nature of the summit of Constitution Hill. Although it is often tempting to nip over to the edge of the cliffs to have a look down, you should be warned that many parts are eroded and crumbling, and there are some very long drops onto very hard rocks. If you decide to walk the nature trail (highly recommended - see above) then note that the guide gives warnings about the more dangerous parts.

Pendinas

OS Maps:	1:50 000 Landranger 135 (Aberystwyth); 1:25 000 Pathfinder 926 (SN 57/58: Aberystwyth).
Start:	Aberystwyth Harbour.
Access:	Aberystwyth is easily reached via the A44 from the east, or the A487 from the north or south. Aberystwyth Harbour is signposted from the town centre.
Parking:	Parking is available at the harbour itself. Alternatively, if parking is difficult during the peak tourist season, it is possible to park at almost any point along the sea front (in which case your walk will be extended slightly as you will have to walk back to the harbour area).
Grade:	Easy - involves just over 100m ascent in total. Well defined paths. Walking boots probably not necessary in summer - training shoes would be quite adequate - although they would be a good idea in winter as some of these paths can get very muddy indeed following wet weather.

Another easy walk, completing our tour of Aberystwyth. This time, we delve back further into Aberyswyth's past with a visit to an Iron Age Celtic hillfort. This walk could be combined with walk 1 to form a grand tour of the town.

Points of Interest:

1. Afon Rheidol. The Rheidol is not one of Wales' most famous rivers, and neither is it one of the longest, but it makes up for these deficiencies with a plethora of glorious scenery that one could imagine producing considerable jealousy in its more famous fellow waterways. Like the Severn and the Wye, the Rheidol rises in the Pumlumon area, and indeed, these three rivers are sometimes referred to as the Three Sisters. According to folklore, these three rivers agreed to rise on Pumlumon early one morning, so that they could pay a visit to the

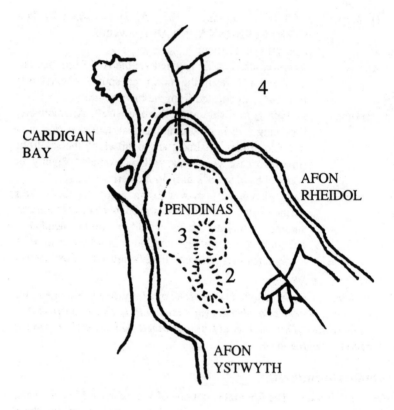

CARDIGAN
BAY

4

1

AFON
RHEIDOL

PENDINAS

3

2

AFON
YSTWYTH

seaside. On the appointed day, the Severn got up earliest, and wound a long and tortuous route down to the sea near Chepstow. The Wye, however, didn't get up quite so early, and had to make a more direct route to the sea to meet her sister, the Severn, near Chepstow. The Rheidol, though, was a lazy so-and-so and had a good, long lie in. By the time she rose, she only had time to make a short, rapid route to the sea, and so had to make for the nearest coastline at Aberystwyth. This legendary laziness apart, however, the Rheidol meanders down from Pumlumon to Aberystwyth along one of the prettiest valleys in Wales, and perhaps the best way to enjoy this glorious countryside is to take a ride on the Vale of Rheidol Railway, the route of one of the famous great little trains of Wales, which runs from Aberystwyth Station to the terminus at Devil's Bridge (see also walk 11).

2. Wellington Monument. This spiky monument, visible from all over Aberystwyth and, no doubt, from miles out to sea as well, was erected to commemorate the Duke of Wellington, famous as the victor in the Battle of Waterloo against the forces of Napoleon Bonaparte (and less famous as a subsequent Prime Minister). I have tried in vain to establish a meaningful link between Wellington and Aberystwyth. None of my history books can help, and neither could the Tourist Information Centre. As far as I know, he wasn't born here, he didn't live here, and he didn't win any battles here, so I suppose he must have come here on his holidays. Perhaps this is a mystery for the reader to try to solve when visiting the town!

3. Pendinas Iron Age Fort. It is said that northern Ceredigion (formally Cardiganshire) boasts no fewer than twenty-nine hillforts, though few of these are well known and none is more frequently visited than this one. Pendinas (the name can be translated a number of ways, though High Fort is probably the most logical) is, in fact, two forts. The northern fort is quite primitive, while the later southern hillfort is more extensive, with triple earthen ramparts. The view from here across Cardigan Bay is spectacular, and the fort must have been a formidable defensive structure (which, given the tendency of the Celts to fight amongst themselves, must have been just as well).

4. Aberystwyth. The main town of the west coast of Wales has a curious name, for Aberystwyth lies not at the mouth of the Ystwyth (as

the name would suggest) but at the mouth of the Rheidol. Originally known as Llanbadarn, the town achieved borough status in 1277. The town of Aberystwyth is an important centre of Welsh culture, for not only is the town itself at the heart of a very strong Welsh-speaking area, but it also boasts two important centres of culture and learning in the University College and the National Library of Wales. The University College of Aberystwyth was the first university institution in Wales, and was paid for essentially by the people of Wales themselves. In the Victorian era, a drive was initiated to start a college in Wales, and money was collected at chapels and at eisteddfodau all over Wales. Together with a few large donations from Welsh industrialists, and other contributions from the Welsh diaspora, the original college building on the sea front (formally a hotel built in the Gothic style) was purchased and, in 1872, it became the University College. This original building still exists, and is still part of the University (you pass the building on walk 1), but these days the college is a much larger institution with a number of buildings across the town, although the main buildings can be seen away to the north east from here. Close by the current main University buildings is the National Library of Wales, built in 1911, that, among many other things, houses a number of priceless old manuscripts including the *White Book of Rhydderch*, a primary source of the tales of the Mabinogion (see walk 3).

Walk Directions:

1. From the harbour, walk north along the sea front to the Harbourmaster's station. You can see Pont Trefechan away to the right. Turn right here, and follow the best way up to the main road (A487). Turn right over Pont Trefechan to cross the Rheidol [1], and continue south along the main road for about 150m until you reach Felin y Môr Road, which heads off quite steeply uphill on the right. Turn right onto this road, then follow it towards the south, past Belvedere on the left, and on until you reach the waymarked footpath on the left that marks the way up to the summit of Pendinas.

2. Take this waymarked footpath uphill. The path is very clear, and it boasts a number of wooden benches affording fine sea views, though it

can be very muddy after a spell of wet weather. In a few places, the path is quite eroded, so care should be taken. The river between Pendinas and the sea is the Ystwyth, and its mouth is situated near the harbour (so I suppose that if you want to be pedantic about this I suppose that this area is the "true" Aberystwyth, while the town of Aberystwyth itself, a little further to the north, should be called "Aberrheidol" - aren't place-names wonderful!). Continue up along this path, taking the sharp left turn close to the top, to the Wellington monument [2] and the Iron Age hillfort [3].

3. At the summit, and during the early stages of the descent from the summit, you will have a good view of the town of Aberystwyth [4]. From the monument, head north across the summit past the remains of the ramparts of the original southern section of the hillfort, before following the obvious path down just north of east. The path soon bears off more or less north downhill back to the main road. Follow the main road back to Pont Trefechan, then return to the start point at the harbour.

Facilities:

As a tourist seaside town, Aberystwyth has all the facilities that you are ever likely to need. From the harbour you can walk along the sea front (as in walk 1), where you will encounter no shortage of ice-cream shops, chip shops, and even Indian and Chinese take-aways. The harbour also boasts a Royal National Lifeboat Institution station, which includes a gift shop. Note that some facilities may be closed during the winter months.

Safety Notes:

As far a navigation is concerned, safety is not much of an issue for this walk - at worst it follows very easily followed paths. There is one safety point, however, concerning the Wellington Monument at the summit of Pendinas. On my last visit - which followed a period of very windy weather - the area immediately surrounding the monument was cordoned off by metal barriers (or at least it would have been if they hadn't blown over). The reason for this was that the storms have produced some damage at the top at the monument - some of the masonry had obviously blown off. Therefore, beware of falling masonry at this place (at least until it is fixed).

·

Pumlumon Fawr - Y Garn

OS Maps:	1:50 000 Landranger 135 (Aberystwyth); 1:25 000 Pathfinder 927 (SN 68/78: Tal-y-bont & Ponterwyd).
Start:	Eisteddfa-Gurig (GR 797 841).
Access:	Start point is on the main A44 Rhayader-Aberystwyth road.
Parking:	Car park at Eisteddfa-Gurig.
Grade:	Strenuous - involves a total ascent of approx 450m. Paths and open moorland. Walking boots essential.

A genuine mountain trek to visit the highest point in Central Wales and to sample one of the three great mountains of Wales. The walk is probably easier than it sounds, but nevertheless gives a real feeling of wilderness and solitude.

Points of Interest:

1. Eisteddfa-Gurig. The name can literally be translated as "The Seat of Curig". It is said that St Curig, a 6th century saint, stopped here to rest on his way from the west coast to the interior of Wales. However, it would appear that he didn't stop here for long, travelling further east to found a church at Llangurig. There are a few buildings here now, and in recent years there has been a cafe with bed and breakfast accommodation at the farmhouse adjacent to the car park. However, this may no longer be the case. On my last visit here, the cafe and bed and breakfast sign had been removed, and there was no sign of life in the farmhouse. While it is possible that these facilities may again be available in the future, it would appear prudent not to rely on them. It should be noted, however, that there is still a sign in the car park asking walkers to pay a parking fee of £1 at the farmhouse, and therefore walkers should at least attempt to pay this toll before setting off up Pumlumon.

2. As the miners' track leads up from Eisteddfa-Gurig to the

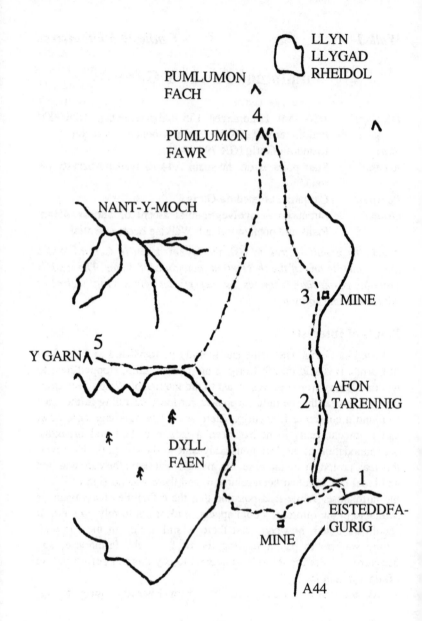

Pumlumon Lead Mine, it should be possible to gain a first glimpse of the red kite population that is to be found inhabiting the area. Since the demise of the golden eagle population of the area in the 1930s, the red kite is perhaps Wales' most spectacular bird and is quite unmistakable with its red-tinged arrow-shaped tail. At the start of the twentieth century, the red kite was all but extinct in this area, but fortunately it has made a very successful come-back and is now common enough to be viewed with some ease around this area as it soars and swoops with imperial grace. Indeed, red kites may well be seen virtually throughout this walk. The red kite also makes a significant contribution to the Welsh tourist industry, as a number of Kite Country Centres have opened across Central Wales, the nearest of which is situated near Ponterwyd (see below).

3. Pumlumon Lead Mine. There are numerous old mine workings in the area - there is another later in this walk near Foel Wyddon (GR 792 839) and others are to be found just south of the main road near Cwmergyr (GR 791 828) and at the old Nantiago Lead Mine east of Cerrig yr Ŵyn (GR 827 863), which was closed in 1920. The Pumlumon Lead Mine was closed in 1895, and on a fine day more than a century later we can only imagine what arduous labour it must have been to extract metal from this exposed landscape. Without the benefits of modern breathable waterproofs, fleece jackets, and twentieth-century technology, and with precious little protection against wind, rain and snow, the Victorian lead miners must have been a hardy breed. It is perhaps an irony that mines such as these, that at first sight appear as eyesores upon the landscape, are now very often protected as industrial heritage sites.

4. Pumlumon Fawr. The writer W. F. Peacock once, rather dramatically, stated that anyone who climbed Pumlumon alone was a fool, for they had but one chance in a hundred of returning safely and ninety-nine chances of never being heard of again. Perhaps nineteenth century writers were a little over-keen on doom and gloom, or perhaps Mr Peacock was just not very good at walking up mountains, but either his description is utter nonsense or my continued existence is little short of a miracle, for this is one of my favourite mountains and one that I never tire of visiting - often alone! At 752m above sea level

it is perhaps surprising that Pumlumon Fawr ranks no higher than Wales' fifty-first highest peak. Yet Pumlumon Fawr is often classed, along with Snowdon and Cadair Idris, as one of Wales' three great mountains, and the magnificent view from the summit is, on a fine day, well worthy of such an accolade. Close by to the north and west, Pumlumon Fach and Drosgol appear as deceptively gentle humps, and deep in the valley the waters of the Nant-y-Moch Reservoir ripple blue and cool - a refreshing thought after a hot climb. To the south the most intriguing view is of Y Garn, whose ridge appears to undulate in ripples, rather like the back of the Loch Ness monster. These ripples will be explored later in this walk. To the north and east lie numerous foothills of the Pumlumon range on either side of the Hengwm valley, and indeed as far as the eye can see in virtually every direction there is wave upon wave of rolling hills ready to entice the map-reader into trying to identify as many tops as possible (I wish you luck!). The summit itself boasts three Bronze Age cairns, although the middle cairn has been somewhat vandalised to form a series of stone shelters. Past excavations on this site have uncovered arrowheads dating back to the Bronze Age, so presumably this area was a hunting ground for the pre-Celtic inhabitants. As the highest point in the Central Wales ranges, it is perhaps fitting that the peak of Pumlumon Fawr is not only close to the sources of two of the great rivers of Wales - the source of the Wye is about one mile to the east (GR 803 870 - you will get a lot closer to this on walk 5) and the source of the Severn is about three miles to the north-east (GR 822 899) - but also offers a unique opportunity to view two great mountains from a single vantage point. On an exceptionally clear day, it is said to be just about possible to see Cadair Idris away to the north and Pen y Fan of the Brecon Beacons away to the south east. The Pumlumon area is also well supplied with mythological references. Pumlumon Fawr itself is mentioned in the Mabinogion, perhaps the greatest collection of Welsh folklore and certainly a classic of medieval literature. The story, from the tale of Culhwch and Olwen, is certainly strange. It was said that Cai and Bedwyr, two of King Arthur's Knights, were on top of Pumlumon one day, when they saw smoke away to the south. The smoke was from a fire stoked for cooking a wild boar, and the cook was none other than

Dillus the Bearded, who was the mightiest warrior ever to have fled Arthur's clutches. Cai's plan was to relieve Dillus of his beard and to make it into a leash to hold Drudwyn the whelp son of Eri - for some reason only the beard of Dillus could make a leash strong enough and the beard had to be removed while the unfortunate warrior was still alive else it would be brittle. So, Cai and Bedwyr let Dillus eat his fill until he was drowsy and fell asleep, then they quietly dug a pit underneath the sleeping warrior so they could hit him over the head and bury him in the pit. This would conveniently keep Dillus immobile so that they could safely pluck out his beard with wooden tweezers. The improbable plan worked perfectly, and having acquired the necessary facial hair the two Knights finished Dillus off, made their leash, and left Pumlumon to go and meet Arthur in Cornwall. It did not seem that Arthur was very impressed, however, as he engaged in some mickey-taking of Cai. This made Cai angry, and henceforth relations between Arthur and Cai were distinctly cool. A strange tale indeed! The name Pumlumon, incidentally, is thought to derive from the word *pump*, meaning five, although it is by no means clear why the word "five" should be so significant in this respect. Perhaps it refers to five peaks (presumably Pumlumon Fawr, Pumlumon Fach, Pumlumon Arwystli, Pumlumon Llygad Bychan and Y Garn, though what about Pencerrigtewion, Pumlumon Cwmbiga and the various others?), or possibly to five rivers (again, presumably the Wye, Severn, Rheidol and two others, although there are many candidates).

* * *

The Mabinogion

It is well known that the Welsh, throughout their history, have had their bards. Indeed, the words of the Welsh national anthem, no less, describe Wales, pretty accurately, as a land famous for its singers and bards. The popular image of the bard is as a poet, though it is no less true that prose, as well as poetry, was the raw material worked and performed by the bards for many hundreds of years, a tradition that is echoed to this day in the National Eisteddfod. However, perhaps the best known stories of the bards of ancient times are collected in the book known as the Mabinogion, and it is always worth reminding ourselves that truly great Western European literature pre-dates Shakespeare and Chaucer by many centuries.

The true origins of the various stories collected in the Mabinogion will probably never be known for sure. It is known that the collection as it exists today is drawn from two fourteenth century manuscripts, the *White Book of Rhydderch* (which is to be found at the National Library of Wales at Aberystwyth) and the *Red Book of Hergest* (which is to be found in the library of Jesus College, Oxford). However, even at this time these stories had undoubtedly been in the repertoire of the bards for a long time, and written fragments of many of the stories have been recovered from manuscripts that pre-date the *White* and *Red* books by at least one hundred years. Some authorities claim that some of the stories in the collection may originate in their modern form in the eleventh century, while others may date even earlier. Even if the date of the authorship of the stories could be established, however, it is still difficult to identify the era in which the stories are set, or from which the ideas contained within them originate. Many would be content to assign the stories to the so-called Golden Age of Welsh history, a time of princes and heroes when the rest of Europe was immersed in the Dark Ages, somewhere between the departure of the Romans from these shores and the arrival of the Normans (or possibly even pre-dating the arrival of the Saxons). Others may assign to the stories an even earlier origin, perhaps stretching back to the very origins of the Celts themselves.

There are eleven tales in the modern collection of the stories of the Mabinogion. As is found in virtually any ancient collection of works, there are clearly different authors for the various stories and they were obviously written at different times, betraying different influences (the same, of course, is true of the Bible). Indeed, although the myths and legends described in the stories are coherent as a body of work, the storylines are not entirely consistent (again, rather like the Bible). Herein are contained the exploits of figures such as Pryderi, Bran the Blessed, and the historical figure of Macsen Wledig. Herein too are some of the earliest - perhaps *the* earliest - expositions of the Arthurian cycle. More than anything else, though, the stories are a masterpiece of language, and little of the beauty is lost via translation into English. Taken together, the stories of the Mabinogion represent the earliest surviving coherent body of literature in any modern European language, and although scholars may argue and dispute the meanings and origins of the tales, none is willing to deny that the authors were anything others than true masters of their craft.

There is insufficient space here even to begin to do justice to the detail and complexity of the tales. They contain myth and legend, they contain heroics and great deeds. Some are solemn, some are funny, and some are downright bizarre. The story of Cai and Bedwyr on Pumlumon Fawr, outlined above, is only one small part of one of the eleven stories of the Mabinogion. We are fortunate in that this rich tapestry of Celtic story-telling is available for all to read and is easily obtainable as a paperback from any decent bookshop. In the end, I can only recommend that you read the stories for yourself.

* * *

5. Y Garn. On the map, Y Garn does not look particularly impressive, but it would be a shame to miss out on the fourth highest top in the Pumlumon range, and on approach it becomes apparent that Y Garn has charms all of its own. It has its frustrations too, not least the "Loch Ness monster humps" alluded to above, for the ridge rising to the summit undulates quite alarmingly, making the ascent in reality rather harder than one might assume from the map. To make things a little more irritating for tired legs, it is not possible to see every "hump" ahead, and it is distinctly annoying to see the Bronze Age summit cairn just ahead, seemingly tantalisingly close, only to realise that more humps must be negotiated before reaching the top. Still, as with all summits, once you have actually reached the top it doesn't seem so bad after all, and the views, particularly to the south across the forest, are stunning. One great advantage of climbing Y Garn after Pumlumon Fawr is that you are able to appreciate the latter as an impressive mountain. The relatively easy climb up the southern slopes of

Pumlumon Fawr can clearly be seen, but also at last the more dramatic northern aspect can be viewed in all its splendour.

Walk Directions:

1. Starting at the car park at Eisteddfa-Gurig [1], make your way to the west of the farmhouse, where a track through the farm will take you to the start of the walk. You will have to cross a stile next to a metal farm gate, and then just ahead there are two more metal farm gates. The one to the left will take you up the south ridge path towards Y Garn (which is the way you will emerge at the end of the walk), while the one to the right leads to the miners' track - it is marked "Plynlimon". Taking this right hand gate, continue up the obvious track, with the noisy, bubbling stream to your right. Ignore the grass covered bridge that appears to the right, and continue forwards for a few metres until you reach the point where the waymarked stony track takes a sharp ninety degree turn to the right and it becomes necessary to ford the stream that is cascading downhill. The easiest way to ford the stream is to continue forwards for about 25 metres or so where it becomes narrower, but the whole area is rather boggy and you must be careful to avoid getting wet feet. Having crossed the stream, now continue up the very obvious miners' track heading north parallel with the river. The Afon Tarennig is really quite spectacular - it may not be a major river, but for the whole length up to the Pumlumon Lead Mine it cascades prettily and noisily, and once you are clear of the farm it really gives the area quite a wild feel [2].

2. Continue up the obvious stony miners' track until another metal gate is reached. Unfortunately, this gate is often locked and there is no stile, so you will probably have to climb over it. The path continues very clearly northwards, giving good views of Pen Pumlumon Llygad Bychan (not marked as such on the map, though this is the 727m spot height near Pen Lluest-y-carn, and it will be visited on walk 5) just east of north, until after a mile or so past the farm the workings of the old Pumlumon Lead Mine [3] come into view. The initial dirty red spoil heaps are not very attractive, but as you continue up the path the ruined buildings and other structures come into view. These are still

not exactly attractive, but they do give a flavour of how unpleasant the occupation of lead miner in Victorian times must have been. At least the Tarennig manages to add a rather nicer note, tumbling carelessly through the old workings. Note that you have a choice of routes as you approach the mine workings. The easiest way up Pumlumon Fawr is to look for the waymark on the left hand side of the path that points you uphill to follow a series of wooden stakes. Alternatively, however, you can proceed to the mine workings themselves, then bear off uphill at this point, rejoining the waymarked path a little further up, as described below. This latter path is perfectly okay, though it can be a bit boggy after a prolonged period of wet weather. If you are worried about getting wet feet, you can always proceed forward to take a look at the mineworkings then double back to the start of the main waymarked path.

3. Beyond the mine, there are a number of paths leading onwards. The most obvious leads off to the north east over a wooden bridge, but the one we want is a very rough, red-tinged, stony path that leads off uphill on a bearing of about 352 degrees from the mine workings. At last Pumlumon Fawr comes into view, although our red stony path soon peters out and it becomes necessary to bear off slightly to the left, though still heading uphill. At this point it should be possible to see the line of wooden stakes to the left heading uphill, and it is towards these stakes that you should head. The going between the red stony path and the line of stakes is a little boggy in places, but it is not too bad, and it should be pretty easy to keep your feet dry in all but the very worst weather. Once you reach the line of stakes, follow it up. The path that follows the stakes flatters to deceive - no sooner does it appear than it fades away again - but the line of stakes is clear enough and takes us up a bit of a pull and on towards the summit. Although this is by no means the most difficult route up Pumlumon Fawr, it is certainly my favourite - it is well worth stopping frequently on the way up to admire the vista to the south. It always seems to me that you only have to move up a few metres at a time to see yet another layer of rolling hills emerging on the horizon, and I like the way that this, one of the great panoramas of Central Wales, unfolds slowly. Just as you think that you must have seen everything, yet more comes into view.

4. As the stakes continue uphill, the path becomes clearer, until eventually the stakes seem to run out just as the upper Tarennig valley opens up in front of us. Pen Pumlumon Llygad Bychan is now a spectacular sight, and the cairn marked on the 1:25 000 map at GR 794 870 lurks mysteriously between this top and Pumlumon Fawr itself. Note the windfarm at approximately 120 degrees. The path now continues very obviously to the summit of Pumlumon Fawr, and although there are still a few more stakes to mark our way, these now give way to small cairns, about two feet high, which will now mark our way to the summit itself.

5. The approach to the summit is oddly flat, and it is difficult to make out the summit itself until you are nearly on top of it. Keep following the small cairns around the rubbly summit area, and eventually a wire fence and the larger Bronze Age summit cairns will come into view. A stile leads across the wire fence to the summit [4]. The trig point is nestled behind one of the larger cairns, and suddenly the breath-taking views north are revealed as Pumlumon Fawr surrenders its last secret. To the west, Drosgol looms majestically over the Nant-y-moch reservoir, but as we saw to the south, so now to the north and west we can view hills rolling away seemingly without end for as far as the eye can see. Budding eco-warriors might like to note that another windfarm is now visible, this time at about 50 degrees, with yet another single windmill at about 335 degrees. It is worth a visit to the most northerly cairn of the three on the summit, although rather disappointingly it is very difficult to get a decent view of Llyn Llygad Rheidol, tucked down to the north. It is, perhaps, possible to feel a little sorry for Pumlumon Fach from this vantage point - it is an impressive hill in its own right, but is doomed to spend eternity being overshadowed imperiously by its big brother. You may like to note that it is possible to see the Irish Sea from this vantage point, over towards Aberdyfi.

6. From the summit of Pumlumon Fawr, it is necessary to strike off slightly west of south, along the ridge (marked Pen y Drawsallt on the 1:25 000 map) towards Y Garn. The path now mostly follows the wire fence, although it is a good idea to make sure you are to the left of the fence as you stride off south. Once again, small cairns mark the way,

though the path is very obvious. The path and the wire fence eventually bring you to the edge of the forestry, and it is now necessary to cross the fence again to head west for Y Garn. Unfortunately, the old stile that used to help you over the fence junction at GR 784 851 is no longer there, and it is necessary to take a little care as you cross the fence, particularly if your inside leg measurement is less than 28 inches! Now it is a straightforward matter to head up the hill to the summit of Y Garn, though rather more strenuous than the map would suggest, as there are a number of steep climbs and sharp dips to be negotiated before the Bronze Age summit cairn is reached [5].

7. From the summit, return east to the fence junction at GR 784 851, then follow the edge of the forestry initially south west, then south (slightly boggy in places but before too long the path improves considerably into a Landrover track) towards the junction of paths at GR 787 840. Here, a path across a stile leads on west into the forest, and a second path proceeds straight forwards south-westish. However, it is the left-hand path leading south of east that we want, which weaves its way towards and past the mine workings at GR 792 839, and back down to the farm at Eisteddfa-Gurig.

Facilities:

As stated above, the cafe and bed and breakfast facilities at Eisteddfa-Gurig may not be available. However, Llangurig (about 8 miles east along the A44) is well provided with tea rooms and bed and breakfast facilities. Devil's Bridge (about 7 miles south west along the A44 and A4120) also has numerous facilities. The Nant yr Arian Forest Centre near Ponterwyd (about 6 miles west on the A44) is designated as a Kite Country Centre, and boasts video pictures of red kites, peregrines and falcons as well as much other bird-related information. (Open 10.00 to 5.00 daily from Easter to the end of September: Tel 01970 890694).

Safety Notes:

Although most of this walk is along reasonably well-defined paths, it is a trek into genuine mountain country, and therefore map, compass, and appropriate clothing should be regarded as essential. In fine weather, navigation is easy. However, when shrouded in mist Pumlumon should not be under-estimated. W. F. Peacock may well have been exaggerating matters (see above), but you would not want to get caught up here, in bad weather without the usual sensible precautions. If severe mist should come down during the ascent, or while on the summit, the safest course would be to retrace your steps to the miners' track, using the cairns and stakes as a guide (if you miss your way, a compass bearing of about 160 degrees should bring you either to the Lead Mine area or to the Afon Tarennig, which you can follow southwards back to Eisteddfa-Gurig). If it mists over during the descent (or as an alternative safety route from the summit), follow the wire fence south to the fence junction at GR 784 851, then skirt south west around the forest boundary to the track junction at GR 787 840. Take the left hand path back to Eisteddfa-Gurig.

Llyn Llygad Rheidol - Pumlumon Fach

OS Maps: 1:50 000 Landranger 135 (Aberystwyth); 1:25 000 Pathfinder 927 (SN 68/78: Tal-y-bont & Ponterwyd).

Start: Junction of minor road with track at GR 768 874.

Access: From the A44 just east of Ponterwyd, take the country lane at GR 751 812, signposted for the Nant-y-moch dam. However, before reaching the dam, take the right turn at GR 763 864 to the start point.

Parking: There should be room to park one or two cars off the road near the start point.

Grade: Strenuous - involves about 325m ascent in total. Tracks and open country. Walking boots essential.

A fine mountain walk, including a trip to the summit of Pumlumon Fawr's little brother, plus a glimpse of several unexpected mountain tarns. The final haul up to the summit of Pumlumon Fach is not long, but quite steep. This route may be treated as an alternative way up to Pumlumon Fawr, as the walk from Pumlumon Fach to Pumlumon Fawr is fairly straightforward.

Points of Interest:

1. Nant-y-moch Reservoir. This reservoir, built between 1957 and 1960 and officially opened in 1964, takes water from a number of rivers, including the Hyddgen and Hengwm, which effectively feed the infant Rheidol which has its source at Llyn Llygad Rheidol (see below). Its function is to provide the water to power the Rheidol Hydro-Electric Scheme. The outflowing waters beyond the dam at GR 75 86 (easily visited by car) form the Rheidol proper.

2. Site of the Battle of Hyddgen, 1401. By the beginning of the fifteenth century, the Welsh rebellion against the English crown, led by Owain Glyndŵr, was in full swing. Attempts by the English King, Henry IV, to crush the rebellion were failing in the face of Welsh

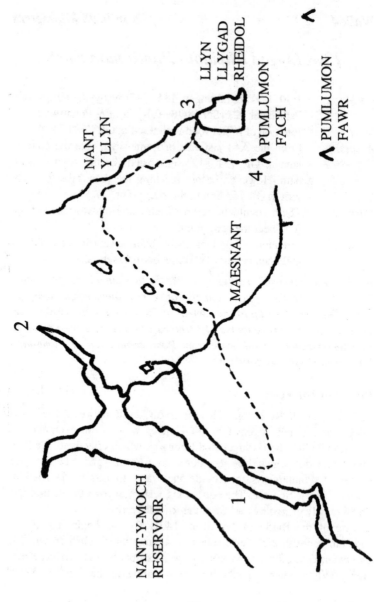

NANT-Y-MOCH RESERVOIR

NANT Y LLYN

LLYN LLYGAD RHEIDOL

PUMLUMON FACH

PUMLUMON FAWR

MAESNANT

1
2
3
4

guerrilla tactics. For the most part, the outnumbered Welsh avoided pitched battles, but in 1401, in the Hyddgen Valley in Pumlumon, a force lead by Owain Glyndŵr were set upon by an army of English and Flemish soldiers some 1500 strong (many of whom were from the Landsker of South Pembrokeshire, and who were set firmly against Owain's goal of a Welsh state independent of England), and a ferocious battle ensued. Heavily outnumbered, Owain's men were surrounded, and were left with no alternative but to fight their way out. The outcome was one of Glyndŵr's most spectacular victories, for the King's men were utterly routed, and before long Glyndŵr would be in control of virtually all of Wales (see below). The site of the battle is commemorated now by a standing stone, which may just about be visible in the Hyddgen valley from this point.

* * *

Owain Glyndŵr

It is difficult to overstate the importance of Owain ap Gruffudd, otherwise known as Owain Glyndŵr, in Welsh history. He is the national hero of heroes, the ultimate symbol of Welsh nationhood, and his significance, perhaps, lies primarily in the sphere of symbolism rather than of his historically verifiable exploits.

He was an unlikely hero. Born into a wealthy Marcher family, he was descended both from Prince Llywelyn and from the ruling family of Deheubarth in South Wales. Yet his early life was unremarkable, and it is something of an irony that he spent much of his life fighting for the English cause in a distinguished, though not particularly spectacular, military career. By the time he reached middle age, Owain was living the life of a retired country gentleman, owning considerable lands around the Dee. At this time, Wales was fully in the control of the English crown. There were gripes, of course, particularly in rural Wales, where the English domination was resented. However, the English King, Richard II, was relatively popular, and there was little outward sign of the rebellion that was to follow.

It was political machinations in England that were to fan the flames of war. Towards the end of the fourteenth century, Richard II was ousted by Henry Bolingbroke, who took the crown to become Henry IV. The new King was far from popular, however, and many of his actions outraged the Welsh, though it was an obscure dispute over land that sparked rebellion. One of the King's henchmen, Lord Grey of Ruthin, unlawfully seized some land in the north east of Wales, and he was backed up in his claim by the King. The former owner of the land was not at all happy about this - this landowner was Owain Glyndŵr.

It is not at all clear at this point what Owain's motivations were. Some said he was being manipulated by the Tudor family, who were later to seize the English throne after the Wars of the Roses. Others said he was working to secure the return to the throne of the ousted Richard II. Nevertheless, by now Owain had abandoned all pretence of loyalty to the despised Henry IV and he set about gathering an army to oppose the King, claiming for himself the title of Prince of Wales. Welsh outrage at the actions of Henry IV were quite sufficient to ensure that Owain enjoyed massive popular support, and Welshmen from all over the country - and from the Welsh diaspora in London and Oxford - flocked to his side.

By 1400, the Welsh were in full rebellion, and marched on several English castles. Henry, of course, had to respond, though Owain's men remained elusive. For most of the rebellion, outright pitched battles were avoided by the Welsh, and guerrilla tactics were the order of the day. For a long time, these tactics were startlingly effective, and by 1406 Owain was in control of virtually the whole of Wales. So successful was Owain that even his enemies started to believe that he was more than human; many believed that he was able to control the weather, as several of Henry's forays into Wales were thwarted not by Welsh military action but by ferocious rainstorms. He established a parliament at Machynlleth, and for the last time in history Wales was effectively a free and independent nation.

It could not last. If nothing else would, then sheer superiority of numbers on the part of the English would prevail, and the small nation of Wales would be slowly ground down and exhausted by an unsustainable effort against superior force. In 1409, Owain lost virtually his entire family when Harlech Castle fell to Henry, and the war was soon won decisively by the English. In 1412, Owain was offered a free pardon by the King, but he refused to take it, and remained a fugitive. It was almost certainly this action that ensured Owain's unique place in history and mythology, for no-one knows what really happened to him after this. It is thought that he died in 1416, at the house of a relative in Herefordshire, but this is uncertain. It was not the destiny of Owain to die and be mourned by his people. Rather, it was his destiny to vanish mysteriously from the historical stage, still clinging to the rightness of his cause, and to become an enduring legend and symbol of Welsh nationhood.

Only King Arthur - who may not have been Welsh at all - is enveloped in more myth and folklore than Owain Glyndŵr. Indeed, perhaps Owain became a latter day King Arthur, and while Owain has no grave that can identified he can be said, by the storytellers and patriots, to be merely sleeping, deep in some Welsh mountain, waiting for the day that he can return and lead Wales, once more, from the domination of England and into its rightful place in the community of nations.

* * *

3. Llyn Llygad Rheidol. This mountain lake-cum-reservoir, which forms the effective source of the Rheidol (although it may be argued that one of the many streams feeding the lake may be regarded as the true source), is tucked away beneath the crags of Graig Las to the east and Pumlumon Fawr to the south, and it is perhaps the one failing of Pumlumon Fawr itself that you cannot get a really good view of Llyn Llygad Rheidol from the summit. However, the lake is easily visible from the initial climb up to Pumlumon Fach, although once again the summit does not allow good views to be had in safety, as the north eastern side of Pumlumon Fach drops almost vertically down to the banks of the lake. In fact, the lake lies within a fabulous natural amphitheatre, enclosed on three sides by Pencerrigtewion, Pumlumon Fawr and Pumlumon Fach. There is a pumping station at the north side of the lake. Note that although it might be tempting for the adventurous to nip across Nant y Llyn to make an assault on

61

Pencerrigtewion (which is slightly higher than Pumlumon Fach, though an easier and less steep climb), this is likely to be dangerous. The nant is just wide enough to make stepping stones necessary, and the only candidates with easy striking distance of Llyn Llygad Rheidol are distinctly dodgy. Be warned!

4. Pumlumon Fach. I have noted elsewhere that one tends to feel rather sorry for Pumlumon Fach, doomed to spend eternity in the shadow of Pumlumon Fawr, but it has its own charms. Just east of north you can see the twin cairns of Banc Llechwedd-mawr, while to the north east Pencerrigtewion stands imperiously, just nine metres higher but seemingly determined to make every centimetre count. To the south east, of course, stands Pumlumon Fawr, while the lesser hump of Pumlumon Fach stands to the east (a detour to this on your way down is fairly straightforward). You may just about be able to see the south side of Nant-y-moch Reservoir poking its head out away to the south west. The summit of Pumlumon Fach, which is dotted with pieces of white quartz, is distinctly bleaker than that of Pumlumon Fawr, having none of the wire fences, large cairns or shelters that adorn the latter. While this gives Pumlumon Fach much more of a feel of isolation and wilderness than its big brother, it also means that the shelter available on the summit of Pumlumon Fawr is not available here. The summit of Pumlumon Fach is not a place to be stranded.

Walk Directions:

1. From the start point in the shadow of Drosgol on the banks on the Nant-y-moch Reservoir [1], follow the obvious track initially south, then north east, around the disused quarries at Bryn y Beddau. The path heads off uphill quite steeply for a while, then it levels out between the unnamed nant north east of Bryn y Beddau and Maesnant. Continue on past the three tarns west of Fainc Ddu.

2. At this point in the walk, you get perhaps the very best views of the Hyddgen Valley away to the north, and you can see from here the site of the Battle of Hyddgen, 1401, down in the valley [2]. After passing Llyn Pen-cor-maen, the track bends round to the east, then heads off south east, shadowing Nant y Llyn to Llyn Llygad Rheidol [3].

3. From Llyn Llygad Rheidol, it becomes necessary to make the tortuous ascent of Pumlumon Fach. There is a paucity of decent paths here, and it is necessary to more or less freelance uphill, somewhere between south and south west. The easiest way uphill is pretty obvious - not least because most of the alternatives look nigh on impossible - and you may be able to make out a very poorly defined path marking the best route (from the point where the track bends to the left at GR 790 879), though it is very steep in parts and care must be taken, especially in less than ideal weather. Following this way up, you will emerge between the two humps of Pumlumon Fach: on the right lies the lower of the two humps (at about 660m above sea level), but the true summit (at 668m) lies atop the hump to your left. Head straight uphill to your left, and you will soon emerge (probably rather breathless) at the summit [4], which is marked by a rather sorry-looking cairn.

4. Pick your way back down to the track leading to Llyn Llygad Rheidol. There are some excellent spots on the way down to eat your sandwiches in comfort - the prevailing winds should be at your back at this point, and the crags provide natural shelter and convenient seats. After regaining the track, it is now a simple matter of re-tracing your steps to the start point, following the track all the way.

Facilities:

There are few facilities in the vicinity. The nearest place to find a shop or a pub is Ponterwyd on the A44. However, as described on walk 3, Llangurig (about a dozen miles east along the A44) is well provided with tea rooms and bed and breakfast facilities. Devil's Bridge (about 3 miles south west along the A44 and A4120) also has numerous facilities. The Nant yr Arian Forest Centre near Ponterwyd is designated as a Kite Country Centre (see walk 3).

Safety Notes:

The final ascent to the summit of Pumlumon Fach on this walk is pretty steep, and walkers would be well advised to make the ascent only in decent weather. Having said that, the well defined track from the start point to Llyn Llygad Rheidol provides few navigational difficulties, and the only problem you are likely to have in this respect is if you get stuck in mist on or near the top of Pumlumon Fach, in which case you are faced with two choices. First, you can re-trace your steps roughly just east of north to the main track, but take great care among the crags. Particularly, take extreme care that you do not wander off route and end up heading for the almost vertical drop to the north down towards Llyn Llygad Rheidol. Personally, although the descent down the craggy path to Llyn Llygad Rheidol can be tricky at the best of times, I would prefer to take this route down - very slowly and very carefully - since the alternative is likely to be inconvenient in the extreme. This is to head south south east to the summit of Pumlumon Fawr, and follow one of the safety routes off there to Eisteddfa-Gurig (see walk 3). This will avoid the worst of the steep crags, but it will take you a long distance out of your way, and you will probably need to summon help to get back to your car on reaching Eisteddfa-Gurig. One other brief point: beware of traffic. It appears that a small handful of locals have decided that it is perfectly alright for them to drive along the track from the start point to Llyn Llygad Rheidol. You can decide for yourself, as you walk the route, the wisdom or otherwise of submitting the average family car to the perils of the journey along this track, but the last time I was there one nutcase decided to drive along it with his two ten or eleven-year-old children on the bonnet. The utter idiocy of such actions can only be marvelled at. Fortunately, such actions are rare, and the route is usually quiet and trouble-free.

Pen Pumlumon Llygad Bychan
- Pumlumon Arlwystli

OS Maps:	1:50 000 Landranger 135 (Aberystwyth & surrounding area); 1:25 000 Pathfinders 927 (SN 68/78: Tal-y-bont & Ponterwyd) and 928 (SN 88/98: Llanidloes).
Start:	Eisteddfa-Gurig (GR 797 841).
Access:	Start point is on the main A44 Rhayader-Aberystwyth road.
Parking:	Car park at Eisteddfa-Gurig.
Grade:	Strenuous - involves a total ascent of approx 450m. Paths and open moorland. Walking boots essential.

If there is one walk in this book that I would recommend above all others, then this is it. A hike out into the heart of the wilderness country of Pumlumon, this walk has the lot: high summits, cavernous valleys, hills rolling away as far as the eye can see, and oodles of peace, quiet and solitude. For a real mountain adventure, it would be possible to combine this walk with walk 3, following the ridge from Pumlumon Arwystli to Pumlumon Fawr, using the wire fence across the ridge as a navigational guide.

Points of Interest:

1. Eisteddfa-Gurig. See walk 3.
2. Pumlumon Lead Mine. See walk 3.
3. Source of the Wye. The Wye is truly one of Wales' great rivers, but even the very greatest of rivers spring from a humble source, and along with its sisters the Severn and the Rheidol, the Wye has its origins in Pumlumon. In fact, if you wish to head down just a little way into the start of the Wye Valley, you may be able to detect the very source itself, which is reported to be beneath a clump of moss branches. The trickle soon becomes a stream, and picks up rapidly as it winds its way through Central Wales, passing through Llangurig,

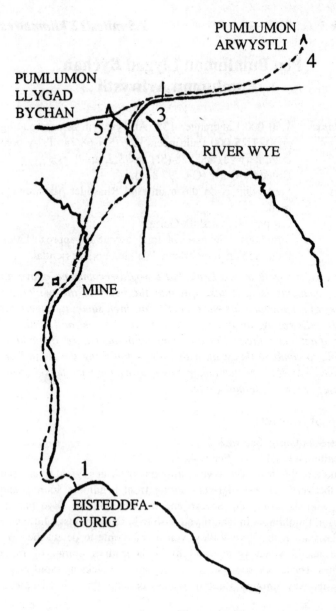

PUMLUMON
ARWYSTLI

4

PUMLUMON
LLYGAD
BYCHAN

5

3

RIVER WYE

2

MINE

1

EISTEDDFA-
GURIG

Rhayader, Builth Wells and Hay-on-Wye, before flirting its way over the border and back again to empty into the Bristol Channel at Chepstow. The beautiful places along the Wye Valley are far too numerous to relate here: suffice it to say that a traveller following the river from the source to the Bristol Channel would experience a veritable A to Z of wonderful walking in Central Wales and the southern Marches.

4. Pumlumon Arwystli. At 741m above sea level, Pumlumon Arwystli is the second highest point in the Pumlumon range, and is only 11m shy of Pumlumon Fawr itself. The summit boasts three Bronze Age cairns, although as on Pumlumon Fawr there has been some mutilation of these cairns to build shelters. The true glory of Pumlumon Arlwystli, however, is the fabulous view from the top. Far away to the north, beyond the Dyfi Valley, you can see the southerly peaks of Snowdonia, and on a good day you should be able to make out Cadair Idris. To the west, meanwhile, the vista is dominated by Pumlumon Fawr, its summit cairns clearly visible, with Pen Pumlumon Llygad Bychan to the south west. To the east, you have a wonderful view of Hafren Forest, while to the south it is possible to catch a glimpse of at least one of the tarns to the south of the A44, and in the far distance you may even be able to see the Claerwen Reservoir (which is certainly visible on a good day from the summit of Pen Pumlumon Llygad Bychan). From the northern part of the summit you may also be able to see Pumlumon Cwmbiga and Carnfachbugeilyn. All in all, a tremendous panorama, and possibly the best in all of the Pumlumon range.

5. Pen Pumlumon Llygad Bychan. This is a slightly mysterious top. The true summit, marked by a cairn at GR 799 872, is not named on the map, though the lower shelf of Pen Lluest-y-carn, also marked by a cairn at GR 801 866, does receive this accolade. In reality, the two places are both part of the overall hill, which, at 727m above sea level, is bested in the area only by Pumlumon Arwystli and Pumlumon Fawr itself. It is a shame that Pen Pumlumon Llygad Bychan doesn't really get the respect it deserves, for this is a nice little summit that affords some excellent views, particularly if you want to see Y Garn, Pumlumon Fawr and Pumlumon Arwystli from a single vantage point.

There is another 1865 boundary stone here (which presumably must have been moved from its original spot, since the county boundary is some way to the east of here). It is not entirely clear whether the cairns around here are Bronze Age or of more recent construction (the ordinary lettering on the OS map would suggest that the cairns are not antiquities), but once again they have been somewhat vandalised to form shelters. On the north east side of the top you may wish to visit a memorial stone. This is a small, slate slab which bears the inscription: *In Memoriam: Alun Llewelyn and Lesley Deane Llewelyn. Their ashes scattered here.* I have no idea who these people were, but they have a beautiful last resting place, in the heart of the most spectacular mountain country in Central Wales.

Walk Directions:

1. Starting at the car park at Eisteddfa-Gurig [1], make your way to the west of the farmhouse, where a track through the farm will take you to the start of the walk. You will have to cross a stile next to a metal farm gate, and then just ahead there are two more metal farm gates. The one to the left will take you up the south ridge path towards Y Garn, while the one to the right leads to the miners' track - it is marked "Plynlimon". Taking this right hand gate, continue up the obvious track, with the noisy, bubbling stream to your right. Ignore the grass covered bridge that appears to the right, and continue forwards for a few metres until you reach the point where the waymarked stony track takes a sharp ninety degree turn to the right and it becomes necessary to ford the stream that is cascading downhill. The easiest way to ford the stream is to continue forwards for about 25 metres or so where it becomes narrower, but the whole area is rather boggy and you must be careful to avoid getting wet feet. Having crossed the stream, now continue up the very obvious miners' track heading north parallel with the river. The Afon Tarennig is really quite spectacular - it may not be a major river, but for the whole length up to the Pumlumon Lead Mine it cascades prettily and noisily, and once you are clear of the farm it really gives the area quite a wild feel. You may also see red kites in this area (see walk 3).

2. Continue up the obvious stony miners' track until another metal gate

is reached. Unfortunately, this gate is often locked and there is no stile, so you may have to climb over it. The path continues very clearly northwards, giving good views of Pen Pumlumon Llygad Bychan (not marked as such on the map, though this is the 727m spot height near Pen Lluest-y-carn and it will be visited later in the walk) just east of north, until after a mile or so past the farm the workings of the old Pumlumon Lead Mine [2] come into view. The initial dirty red spoil heaps are not very attractive, but as you continue up the path the ruined buildings and other structures come into view. These are still not exactly attractive, but they do give a flavour of how unpleasant the occupation of lead miner in Victorian times must have been. At least the Tarennig manages to add a rather nicer note, tumbling carelessly through the old workings.

3. Beyond the mine, there are a number of paths leading onwards. The most obvious leads off to the north east over a wooden bridge, and this is indeed the path that we want. Cross the bridge, and carry on up the path, which heads roughly east from the mine, passing a sheep pen on the left. The summit of Pen Pumlumon Llygad Bychan is now more or less due north. Continue along the path, which gradually becomes more grassy and less distinct as you approach a couple of wooden stakes on the left. By now, Pumlumon Fawr is obvious to the left, while Pumlumon Arwystli comes into view ahead.

4. From here, the easiest way forward is to head more or less straight in the direction of Pumlumon Arwystli until you come to the wire fence, marked on the 1:25 000 OS map, to the east of Pen Lluest-y-carn. By now it will start to become obvious that to continue heading straight for Pumlumon Arwystli is not a good idea, as you would have to drop down into the young Wye Valley. It is vastly easier to turn north to continue following the fence towards and past Pen Lluest-y-carn, then keep following the fence as it turns to the east around the head of the Wye Valley. Note that as the fence veers to the east, you are now within a matter of metres of the source of the Wye [3]. Incidentally, although it is an easy matter to cross the fence if necessary, it is easier all the way along to stick to the west (and later north) side of the fence, as there are well trodden paths on this side that make the walking easier.

5. As the fence veers east, it now takes you onto the ridge between Pumlumon Fawr and Pumlumon Arwystli, and therefore you do not have to lose much height to reach the latter. Continue east and then north east, still following the fence, towards Pumlumon Arwystli. The views from this ridge are very nearly as good as those from Pumlumon Arwystli itself, as you have the Wye Valley to the south and Cwm Gwerin to the north. You should also see a boundary stone marked with the date of 1865, which marks the boundary between Cardiganshire (modern Ceredigion) to the west and Montgomeryshire (modern Powys) to the east. As you approach Pumlumon Arwystli you will reach a collection of prominent peat banks, and you should see a very obvious path veering away from the fence and up to the summit. Make for this path, and the summit is attained after a short pull [4].

6. From the summit of Pumlumon Arwystli, re-trace your steps back down to the fence, and return to the vicinity of Pen Pumlumon Llygad Bychan and Pen Lluest-y-carn [5]. It is but a short detour to bag this summit. Next you have a choice of two routes back to the Pumlumon Lead Mine. In mist, by far the easiest way is to head east back down to the fence, then to follow this downhill to the fence junction at GR 802 860, before doubling back just south of west to the mine. However, if the weather is clear then there is no obstacle to taking a direct route downhill from the summit of Pen Pumlumon Llygad Bychan direct to the mine. It is a little steep in places, and you might have to weave around a bit to avoid the boggier bits (easily recognisable by the reeds that surround them), but it is not difficult and it will allow you to enjoy the upper Tarennig Valley and to observe a ruined stone building (part of the mine workings) that is not observable from the miners' track.

7. From the mine, it is a simple task to return to the start point down the miners' track.

Facilities:

As stated in walk 3, the cafe and bed and breakfast facilities at Eisteddfa-Gurig may not be available. However, Llangurig (about 8 miles east along the A44) is well provided with tea rooms and bed and breakfast facilities. Devil's Bridge (about 7 miles south west along the

A44 and A4120) also has numerous facilities. The Nant yr Arian Forest Centre near Ponterwyd (about 6 miles west on the A44) is designated as a Kite Country Centre, and boasts video pictures of red kites, peregrines and falcons as well as much other bird-related information. (Open 10.00 to 5.00 daily from Easter to the end of September: Tel 01970 890694).

Safety Notes:

Although Pumlumon Arwystli is way out in the middle of wild mountain country, the wire fences that criss cross the area provide very handy navigational tools and make the task of finding your way around this wilderness, particularly in mist, an awful lot easier than would otherwise be the case. If blanket mist should descend while you are around Pumlumon Arwystli, the safest way back to Eisteddfa-Gurig is to head south east off the top until you come to the fence, then follow the fence to the first junction of fences at GR 802 873 and on to the second junction of fences at GR 801 870, then head north west along the fence to the summit of Pen Pumlumon Llygad Bychan before continuing just south of west along the fence to the summit of Pumlumon Fawr. From this summit, follow the fence just west of south along Pen y Drawsallt to the edge of the forest east of Y Garn, then follow the forest and footpaths round to the south east and back to Eisteddfa-Gurig. If stranded around Pen Pumlumon Llygad Bychan or Pen Lluest-y-carn, the most certain way back is to head east until you hit the fence, then follow the fence as above via Pen Pumlumon Llygad Bychan and Pumlumon Fawr back to Eisteddfa-Gurig. Alternatively, you could head south south west across the open country - so long as you keep going down you should hit the Tarennig Valley which will guide you back to the miners' track to return to Eisteddfa-Gurig. However, although this route is shorter and easier, you will not have the security of a fence to follow.

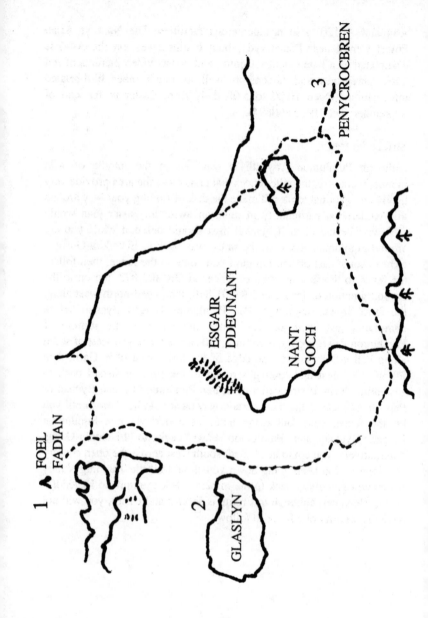

1 FOEL FADIAN

2 GLASLYN

ESGAIR DDEUNANT

NANT GOCH

3 PENYCROCBREN

Foel Fadian - Glaslyn - Penycrocbren
Roman Fortlet

OS Maps:	1:50 000 Landranger 136 (Newtown, Llanidloes & surrounding area); 1:25 000 Pathfinder 907 (SN 89/99: Penffordd-Las).
Start:	Junction at GR 837 952 (east of Foel Fadian).
Access:	The easiest way to the start point is via Llanidloes off the A470. The A470 itself by-passes Llanidloes, though the latter is clearly signed on the B4518. Pass through Llanidloes, and continue along the B4518 following signs for Staylittle. After passing through Staylittle, take the next turning on the left signed for Dylife. Pass through Dylife, and watch out for the junction marking the start point - it bears a sign for a nature reserve, so should be easy to identify.
Parking:	There is just about room to park a car or two at the start point, though be careful not to block access to the Landrover track leading to Glaslyn. If parking is difficult here, there is also room to park a couple of cars at the junction at GR 847 943, though again be careful not to block access.
Grade:	Moderate - involves about 240m ascent in total. Bridleways and open countryside. Walking boots essential - can be boggy in places.

A varied ramble around the northern reaches of Pumlumon, taking in some Roman remains, a mysterious lake, a pretty little hill and the site of an execution! There are also some picturesque valley scenes to be enjoyed.

Points of Interest:

1. Foel Fadian. At 564m above sea level, Foel Fadian fails to

challenge the higher peaks of Pumlumon and the Radnor Forest, but it is a splendid little mountain all the same. I have seen one writer describe Foel Fadian as the sort of small mountain you would like to put in your pocket and take home with you, and I can see what he means. The view to the north and north west of the more southerly peaks of the Snowdonia National Park is particularly striking, although the view to the south also gives a good idea of the splendours of Pumlumon. Glaslyn is shown in all its glory, while you can also see very clearly the bridleways that will take you down and past Glaslyn. I know of no other hill in Central Wales that gives such a great viewpoint as Foel Fadian for (relatively) so little effort, though I must be completely honest here and say that if I could take any hill in Mid Wales home and put it on my mantelpiece it would be Whimble (see walk 13) - though Foel Fadian comes a close second!

2. Glaslyn. Even if you do not take the detour down to the banks of the lake, it is not difficult to appreciate the rather mysterious atmosphere of Glaslyn, particularly if there is a hint of mist in the air. One legend concerning this lake holds that beneath the waters of Glaslyn there is a submerged village, and that all the buildings of the village still exist hidden from view. I do not know whether anyone has ever dived down into the lake to check if the legend is true, though presumably there is no-one still living there!

3. Penycrocbren Roman Fortlet. I find the idea of a Roman "fortlet" quite intriguing. One wonders whether it was full of rather small Roman soldiers, or perhaps there were only a few legionaries here, teeth chattering in the bleak countryside in the middle of nowhere. In fact, excavation has demonstrated that the fortlet was probably built in the early part of the second century A.D. after the conquest of Wales had more or less been completed. However, just to be on the safe side, the Romans were in the habit of leaving small forces of troops dotted around at strategic points, and it is possible that this was one of them. An alternative possibility is that a small force was left here to keep an eye on the lead mine workings nearby, as it is known that lead mining was carried out in this area even in Roman times. Indeed, lead mining was to continue for some centuries, and the village of Dylife (which you passed through on your way to the start point of this walk) grew

up around the industry. The name of the area - Penycrocbren - literally means "Gallows Top" or "Gibbet Top" (the "top" in this context essentially meaning "hill"), and it is thought that this name originates from the eighteenth century execution here of a murderer from Dylife. A skull and gibbeting irons were discovered here in 1938.

Walk Directions:

1. At the start point you have a wonderful view of Foel Fadian, with the trig point on top, and you can also get a tempting glimpse of Glaslyn, so the initial direction to walk in should not be a problem. Head south westish down the Landrover track (signposted as a bridleway and as part of the Glyndŵr Way), until it veers right, and then left just beyond a cattle grid. At this point on the 1:25 000 map there is a footpath marked by a black dotted line heading more or less due west in the general direction of the summit of Foel Fadian, but in truth the path is not very distinct, and indeed there are a multitude of sheep tracks around here to confuse the unwary. The simplest way to make your way up to the summit of Foel Fadian is probably to head as directly as possible for the trig, picking your way across the grassy tussocks - which can be quite boggy after wet weather - using sheep tracks wherever possible to make the going a little easier.

2. On approaching the summit, the trig disappears from view so you will simply need to keep heading upwards, taking care over the rather slippery rocky patches. Finally, after a sharp climb, the trig point is seen again and you have reached the summit of Foel Fadian [1] with its spectacular views. After drinking in the panorama, you will need to head down again, south eastish, and back to the Landrover track heading southish to Glaslyn - it is likely that the easiest way down will be more or less the same way you came up, although you can avoid some boggy bits by tending south to hit the bridleway that skirts the north precipice of Uwch-y-coed. This bridleway also gives the best views down into the forbidding rocky valley of Uwch-y-coed. Beware, however, of the boggier parts of the track - after wet weather in particular sections of this track can be quite flooded, and you will need to skirt around them very carefully to avoid wet feet. Beware, also, of the rockier parts, which can be very slippery.

3. Eventually you will re-join the Landrover track leading southish towards and past Glasyn [2] - it is possible to take a short detour to the banks of the lake itself if you wish, using the track leading down from the 477m spot point on the 1:25 000 map near a cattle grid not marked on the map. As you pass Glaslyn you will come to the first part of the walk where the map can be rather confusing. There is a bridleway leading off to the left at GR 830 939, although this is not at all obvious on the ground and I suspect it merely leads off across the open country. It is much easier to continue to the far more obvious junction of tracks at GR 828 937, and to take the left fork leading just east of south at first, and soon heading off slightly north of south east. This soon rejoins the marked bridlepath, and heads off along Nant Ddu.

4. Now we are back on track, heading downhill to the sheep enclosures at GR 837 930. The bridleway marked on the map heads straight through these enclosures, but it is far better to skirt around the left hand side of them and on down, over a stile, to the wooden footbridge over the young Clywedog. Having crossed over the river, the path to the right up and around the hill is fairly obvious, and soon you come to a fork in the path. The right hand fork skirts around the perimeter of the small gorge leading down to the Clywedog, but we want the left hand fork, which heads away uphill from the gorge and over Y Grug. The path continues reasonably distinctly for a while, passing through a gate at GR 841 932 (there may be a stile here too - the last time I was here it looked like somebody had laid out the component parts of a stile as if ready for construction) but eventually it peters out just short of the fence at a point a little bit north of GR 847 935.

5. This is now, from a navigational point of view, the most difficult part of the walk. The general direction to head in easy enough - more or less due east - but unfortunately the bridleways marked on the map do not appear very obvious on the ground, and to make things worse there are no stiles over the wire fencing to make the going easier. The simplest course of action, on arriving at the fence, is to follow the line of the fence south east for about 50m or so, to the point where there is a triangular junction of fences at GR 847 935. Now follow the line of the fence south west for about 100m to another junction of fences at GR 847 934 (this is more or less whether the more southerly of the two

apparent, but non-existent, bridleways meets the fence on the map). Here, the right-of-way crosses the fence to head more or less due east along a curious bank. Unfortunately there is no stile, so you will have to take your chances crossing the wire fence. Now follow this bank eastish until it veers off to the left. Continue east, however, to the next fence, where a gate will allow you pass through the fence and to a junction of obvious tracks at GR 851 934. This is where the map shows a crossroads of bridleways, and at last we are again back on track. Follow the stony track east of north to another junction of bridleways at GR 852 936, this time marked with finger post waymarks.

6. Take the path east uphill for about 300m or so, where a series of small mounds will signal the site of the Penycrocbren Roman Fortlet [3]. Then, retrace your steps to the last junction of bridleways at GR 852 936. Now follow the bridleway roughly north west up to the road - this section is a part of the Glyndŵr Way long distance footpath. On reaching the road at GR 847 943, head uphill north west and back to the start point.

Facilities:

Very little is available locally - the nearest town of appreciable size is Llanidloes, where shops, pubs and bed and breakfast facilities can be found. There are a few camping sites in the area - you will pass them on your way to the start point. Llyn Clywedog is also worth a visit while you are in the area. You will also pass this on the way to the start point, and there are a number of car parks dotted around it. The car park at GR 921 881 also has public conveniences and picnic tables.

Safety Notes:

Since a significant portion of this walk is across more or less open countryside, navigation in mist may present a few problems. Fortunately, though, the road is never too far away, and as a last resort a compass set to north east must bring you sooner or later to the road, so you can never be completely lost. If blanket mist should descend while you are on Foel Fadian, a compass set to between south east and east should bring you out on the obvious bridleways that will take you back to the road and your car - the main hazard here is to avoid the dramatic drops around Uwch-y-coed, though since these are fairly well fenced off the sensible walker should have no problem. The other potential problem area in mist is around Y Grug, where the paths peter out and one is in open country. However, a compass set to east must again bring you out at the very obvious bridleways to the west of Penycrocbren, which will take you north and north west back to the road. Around this area, avoid drifting to the south, where there is a steep drop down to the Clywedog.

Clap yr Arian - Maen Serth
- Maengwyngweddw

OS Maps:	1:50 000 Landranger 147 (Elan Valley & Builth Wells); 1:25 000 Pathfinders 948 and 969 (SN 87/97: Llangurig & the River Wye and SN 86/96: Rhayader).
Start:	A lay-by situated just south east of the junction of the bridleway leading from Maengwyngweddw with the minor road leading from Rhayader to Aberystwyth (at about GR 923 706).
Access:	Easiest access is via Rhayader, which lies on the A470 between Builth Wells and Newtown. At the junction in the centre of Rhayader, take the B4518 signposted for the Elan Valley, then at Llansanffraid-Cwmdeuddwr turn right onto the Aberystwyth Mountain Road. The start point is roughly three miles along this road.
Parking:	It should be possible to park several cars at the lay-by at the start point.
Grade:	Easy - involves less than 100m ascent in total. Bridleways and good footpaths. Walking boots recommended, especially after wet weather.

A stroll back to the Bronze Age - and a twelfth century murder. This walk could be combined with walk 8 to provide a real marathon hike.

Points of Interest:

1. Clap yr Arian. This Bronze Age barrow (whose name, rather unromantically, translates as Silver Lump), lies to the left hand side of the track at GR 936 699. It may also be viewed, perhaps to better effect, from the higher track between Maen Serth and Maengwyngweddw. It is roughly sixteen metres or so across, with a number of bumps on its southern aspect that Cadw suggests may be the spoil heaps from an early archaeological dig at the site which

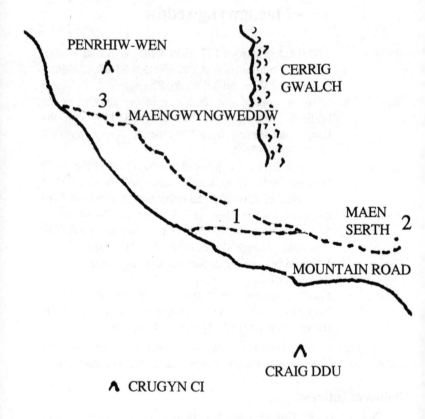

PENRHIW-WEN

CERRIG
GWALCH

MAENGWYNGWEDDW

MAEN
SERTH

MOUNTAIN ROAD

CRAIG DDU

CRUGYN CI

unearthed a Bronze Age battle-axe made of spotted blue dolerite. This is particularly interesting as this material is characteristic of the Preseli mountains in Pembrokeshire, from which the famous blue stones were hewn and transported to Wiltshire for the construction of Stonehenge. It has been suggested, therefore, that the barrow may represent the grave of one of the people responsible for the construction of that most famous megalith. The battle-axe in question may be viewed at the National Museum of Wales in Cardiff.

2. Maen Serth. This striking standing stone has attracted a number of local myths, though as ever it is often difficult to tell where history becomes myth. The stone, made of local shale, is just over two metres tall, and is about half a metre or so across at the base. There is a roughly carved cross on the south side, suggested by Cadw (the body responsible for Welsh ancient monuments) to be of 7th-9th century AD origin, though it is likely that the stone itself, probably Bronze Age in origin, had already been standing for many hundreds, if not thousands, of years. The most popular local story surrounding the stone is that the inscribed cross was added as a memorial to the local chieftain Einion Clud, who was murdered somewhere nearby. According to the tale, Einion had upset a local Marcher Lord by the name of Roger Mortimer by unseating him at a jousting tournament at Cardigan. Mortimer, it seems, was not a good loser, and got his revenge by ambushing the unfortunate Einion and killing him. This was not a popular move with the locals, who inscribed Maen Serth with a cross as a memorial, and even today the stone is known locally as the Prince's Grave. This is certainly a great story, though there are two drawbacks to accepting its authenticity. First, although it seems pretty well established that Mortimer did indeed murder Einion, it is by no means clear where he did so or where the latter is buried. Maengwyngweddw (to be visited later in the walk), to the north west, is at least as good a candidate for the evil deed as Maen Serth. Second, the date of the murder is established as being around Christmas in 1176, which does not tally with the date accepted by Cadw as being the probable date of origin of the inscription. Anyway, there is little doubt that Roger Mortimer was a rather nasty piece of work. Apart from murdering Einion Clud, he also murdered Einion's brother

Cadwallon three years later, whilst he was supposed to be ensuring Cadwallon's safe conduct back to Wales from the court of Henry II. All this skulduggery on Mortimer's part, however, didn't seem to do him any harm - his descendants ascended to the Marcher Lordship regardless, and for the most part were not so bad to their tenants as the wicked Roger.

3. Maengwyngweddw. This unusual Bronze Age standing stone is made of white quartz, hence the name which translates as the White Widow Stone. It is relatively small, being less than a metre in height and slightly larger across, thus having a peculiarly squat appearance (in really bad mist it may be mistaken for a sheep!). As discussed above, this, rather than Maen Serth, may mark the place of the murder of Einion Clud by Roger Mortimer.

Walk Directions:

1. From the start point, walk south east down the mountain road for about three-quarters of a mile until you reach the bridleway signposted off to the left at GR 931 699. Turn left onto this bridleway, heading east.

2. Follow this fairly clear path uphill for about 800m, until you arrive at the junction of tracks at GR 939 699 just after passing the site of Clap yr Arian [1] on the left. Join the larger bridleway, still heading east, until Maen Serth comes into view. Head for this standing stone [2]. Excellent views are to be had, from this area, of the descent down towards the Elan Valley and Rhayader away to the south east, while Craig Ddu and Crugyn Ci dominate the vista to the south west (see walk 8).

3. Return along the bridleway to the junction at GR 939 699. On approaching this junction, it appears that there are three paths to choose from. The one on the left is the way you walked up from the mountain road, while the one on the right heads off uphill to the north. We want the one in the middle, that heads off roughly north west, passing Clap yr Arian on the left.

4. Continue along the bridleway, which is very well defined, to Maengwyngweddw [3], which is to the right of the track and may be

partially obscured by vegetation. From Maengwyngweddw, it is a simple matter to continue along the track until it meets the mountain road, then turn left to walk along the road to the start point.

Facilities:

The nearest facilities are to be found in the town of Rhayader, which is well supplied with places to stay and to eat and drink. The Tourist Information Centre in Rhayader should be able to supply up-to-date information regarding the availability of local accommodation. (See walk 8 for more details).

Safety Notes:

Navigation for this walk should be a piece of cake. The bridleways are extremely well defined throughout. In case of difficulty, following a bearing of south west will bring you quickly back to the mountain road.

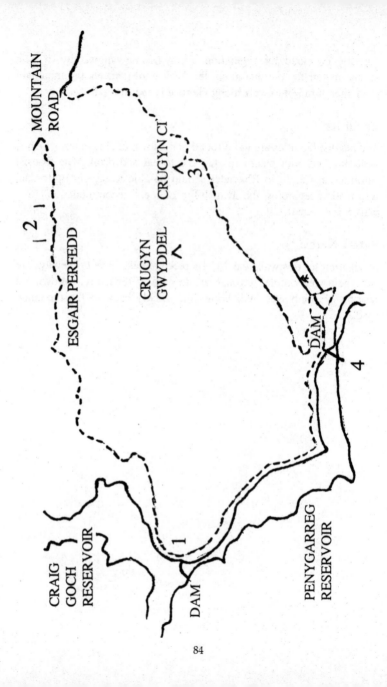

CRAIG GOCH RESERVOIR

DAM

ESGAIR PERFEDD

MOUNTAIN ROAD

CRUGYN GWYDDEL

CRUGYN CI

DAM

PENYGARREG RESERVOIR

1

2

3

4

Esgair Perfedd - Crugyn Ci

OS Maps: 1:50 000 Landranger 147 (Elan Valley & Builth Wells); 1:25 000 Pathfinder 969 (SN 86/96: Rhayader).

Start: Craig Goch Dam (GR 894 687). This is my preferred start point for the walk, as it enables you to gain height early in the walk. However, should parking prove difficult here there is an alternative start point at the Penbont car park near the Penygarreg Dam (GR 915 673). To join the walk from here, cross over the hump-backed bridge to the telephone box, where there is a stile leading to some of the numerous short trails in the area. Cross the stile and follow the waymarked path to the left, through the woodland and over the wooden bridge, to steps leading right up to the top of Penygarreg dam. This leads you a bridleway that forms part of the Elan Valley Trail, and onto the walk as described below.

Access: From Rhayader town centre, follow the B4518 (signed for the Elan Valley) past the Visitor Centre and round to Craig Goch Dam. Turn right here to cross the dam to the start point.

Parking: There is room to park a number of cars at the east end of the dam, which marks the end of the Elan Valley Trail. See above for a possible alternative.

Grade: Moderate to strenuous - involves a total ascent of approx 325m. Bridle paths and open moorland. Walking boots strongly recommended.

A good trek, taking in the atmosphere of the beautiful Elan Valley and following a part of the Elan Valley Trail. One wonders whether the Romans of Esgair Perfedd found the area as wonderful as the modern day walker.

Points of Interest:

1. Craig Goch Dam. The dam is 156m long, 32m thick at its base, and rises some 36m above the river bed, allowing the reservoir a capacity of about two thousand million gallons over an area of 217 acres. It was built as part of the Elan Valley scheme of reservoirs at the end of the Victorian era, and opened on July 21st 1904 by King Edward VII. The water supplied by this scheme is intended primarily to supply the needs of the city of Birmingham, although some is utilised locally. The reservoir produced by the Craig Goch Dam is actually a holding pen, designed to keep the main reservoir further south at Carreg Ddu topped up when necessary. Water from Carreg Ddu is then filtered and transported the 73 miles (118 km) to the Frankley Reservoir at Birmingham. These days, the management of the water scheme falls under the responsibilities of Dŵr Cymru (Welsh Water), who essentially sell on the water to Severn Trent, the water authority covering the Birmingham area, although Severn Trent retain responsibility for the filtering beds and the aqueduct system used for transporting the water to Birmingham.

* * *

Water, water everywhere!

If asked about their impressions of Wales, many people would, no doubt, respond with three things - sheep, rain and rugby (and probably in that order!). It can hardly be disputed that there are a great many sheep in Wales - about three for every human being - and the passion of the nation for the game of rugby union is well documented. But what about the old chestnut that it always rains in Wales? Is there a grain of truth in this? And does this have any relevance for the way that the history of Wales has developed?

Like most received wisdom, the idea that it rains a lot in Wales is not entirely true and not entirely false. In fact, the average rainfall across Wales varies considerably as a consequence of its geography and particularly of its hills, and, like the south west of England, the general climate of Wales is heavily influenced by its geographical position on the western edge of Europe. The prevailing winds here blow from the south west and so much of our air arrives at our shores from the Atlantic Ocean. As a consequence, this air tends to be mild in temperature, so the southern and western parts of Wales tend to have relatively mild climates compared to the east of England or Scotland. This air is also quite moist, so Wales as a whole tends to have more rainfall than the eastern side of England (where the dreaded hosepipe ban is much more common). However, the amount of rain that falls also depends on the topography of the region, particularly on whether or not hills are present. Thus, the great southern cities of Cardiff and Swansea, which are exposed on the coast, enjoy an annual rainfall of roughly 45 inches or so each year. However, as the south westerlies move inland they encounter hills, of which there are more than a few in Wales! The hills force the clouds higher where they get colder, and as cold air does not retain moisture as well as warm air it is found that rainfall can be considerably higher in inland hilly areas. The Elan Valley is a great example of this - rainfall here can be as high as 72 inches per year, making the area a prime candidate for the construction of reservoir systems. As the winds move further east over land the moisture content of the air declines (which is why eastern England tends to be drier than Wales), but there are other factors that may come into play as well. For example, if a town is situated close to the leeward side of a hill, then clouds may be forced up by the presence of the hill and pass high over the town, reducing the rainfall experienced by that town (this happens in the case of Wrexham in north east Wales, which gets barely 30 inches of rain per year) - in which case the town is said to be in a rain shadow. In general terms, though, the direction of the prevailing winds off the Atlantic and the mountainous nature of the terrain means that Wales does indeed tend to get more rainfall than eastern England.

The moist, temperate climate has, of course, had its impact on the history of Wales. In broad terms, many parts of Wales are well suited to agriculture, including vast tracts of Central Wales. There has, therefore, been a tendency for much of the population to earn a living through farming, and necessarily this has had an impact on Wales' social history. In more recent times, though, the ability of Wales to provide drinking water for the general population - and particularly for the drier parts of the U.K. east of Offa's Dyke - has provided a few touchy moments surrounding the building of reservoirs. Indeed, the construction of the Elan Valley water management scheme itself was not met with universal local praise at the time. It necessitated the flooding of considerable tracts of land, the building of Elan Village, and an influx of many of the workers on the scheme from England - and all to provide water for a big English city many miles away. Unfortunately, the necessity to show sensitivity to local feeling in the building of such schemes was not a lesson of history learned by another English city, this time Liverpool. In the 1960s, the Liverpool City Corporation used the mechanism of compulsory purchase order to buy up large areas of the Tryweryn valley in southern Snowdonia, which it used to build a large reservoir. In the process, a village and a number of farms were flooded, and many families were forced to move unwillingly. There was great local resentment and opposition to the scheme, and so strong was the feeling in some quarters that individuals operating under the banner of the Free Wales Army and the Mudiad Amddiffyn Cymru (Movement for the Defence of Wales) carried out a programme of economic disruption, blowing up several transformers and pipelines perceived to be of economic benefit to England at the expense of Wales.

So, water has played a major part in the history of Wales - and continues to fall from the sky in quantities that might please the farmers and gardeners but which occasionally provides a damp day for walkers!

* * *

2. Esgair Perfedd Roman Camp. Unfortunately for the walker, the site does not present a magnificent tableau of Roman remains - in fact at first sight it appears to present nothing at all! The area of the camp is quite clear from aerial photography, though, and a scramble around the site does reveal a few suggestive banks and openings, but there is little that is obvious to grab the attention. The camp was temporary in nature, though quite large (about 15 acres or so) and capable of

accommodating a force of around 4,000 soldiers. It has been suggested that the camp may have served as a stopping point for Roman forces moving north west during the conquest of this area of Wales in the mid to late first century AD.

3. Crugyn Ci. At 533m (1749 ft) above sea level, the summit of Crugyn Ci hardly ranks as one of the great mountains of Wales, yet it affords some terrific views in all directions. To the east, the town of Rhayader nestles snugly in the junction of the Wye and Elan Valleys, while to the south the vista is dominated by the Cwmdeuddwr hills. Far away to the north west, it is supposed to be possible to see Pumlumon Fawr from here, while to the south the Brecon Beacons are also reputed to be visible in good weather. Even in less than perfect conditions, however, the gently rolling hills of the Cambrian ranges are visible in all directions, and about 1 km to the west the cairn of Crugyn Gwyddel is unmistakable (a short side trip to visit this is fairly easy, from whence you can head south to rejoin the bridlepath down to Penygarreg Farm).

4. Penygarreg Dam. The dam is 161m long, 36m thick at its base, and rises 37m above the river bed, allowing the reservoir a capacity of about 1,330 million gallons over an area of 124 acres. Like the Craig Goch Dam, it was built as part of the Elan Valley scheme of reservoirs at the end of the Victorian era that was opened on July 21st 1904 by King Edward VII, and its reservoir is really a holding pen, designed to keep the main reservoir further south at Carreg Ddu topped up when necessary. See the notes for Craig Goch Dam above for further information.

Walk Directions:

1. From the start point, take the bridleway uphill heading north along the Craig Goch Reservoir, before it tends north of east and moves away from the reservoir banks. After about 1 km, the path veers sharp left to a ford which is easy to cross, then right again heading uphill north eastish.

2. Continue to follow the bridleway uphill in the direction of Esgair Perfedd. About 1 km or so beyond the ford the path flattens out somewhat, and becomes increasingly indistinct and difficult to follow,

until a very boggy patch is reached at the apparent "chicane" in the bridle path on the map at GR 911 698. Here, the path seems to peter out altogether, but keep heading north east for about 50m or so (noting the windfarms in the distance east of north), until the path bearing more or less due east once again becomes obvious. It heads slightly uphill for a while, before flattening out at Esgair Perfedd and then turning downhill towards the road. As the path begins to flatten out you can gain your first sight of Crugyn Ci away to the south east.

3. Before reaching the road, the path crosses the site of a temporary Roman encampment at Esgair Perfedd [2] before veering left to an impressive complex of sheep-pens and a ford. The easiest way across the ford is to walk a few metres to the right, where the stream is narrow enough to jump across without difficulty. Having crossed the ford, proceed to the road and turn right.

4. Follow the road for about 300m until a weir off to the right (GR 932 698) marks the way to return via Crugyn Ci. Take one of the paths off right down to the weir. Do not try to cross the weir - there is no continuous way across and to attempt to cross it would be extremely dangerous. Instead, walk downstream for about 50m or so to a large rock on the bank. This will allow you to cross the stream fairly easily. The course of the bridleway leading uphill between south and south east is now very obvious, and you should follow this path uphill past the crags on your right, noting the unexpectedly majestic dome of Craig Ddu to your left and the standing stone of Maen Serth on the skyline somewhat north of east (which is visited on walk 7).

6. Continue uphill on the bridleway to the point where the path veers sharp right on the map (GR 934 694). Unfortunately, the main path becomes indistinct around here, and it is easy to miss this right turn. However, the walking is fairly easy in this area and to miss this turn is not a major problem. Quite simply, if you reach the point where the summit of Craig Ddu is due east then you have missed the turning, and will have to change direction to just south of west towards the craggy slopes of Crugyn Ci. This will bring you back to the bridleway that skirts around Crugyn Ci, now fairly obvious once again. Continue along the path, tending to the south west, until the tiny tarn at GR 931 688 comes into view on the left. Although it is possible to head for the

summit of Crugyn Ci at any point here, perhaps the easiest way is to continue along the bridleway until the tarn is no longer visible, then strike off uphill to the west, using the numerous sheep tracks to make the going over the tussocks and the heather a little easier. After a short but stiffish climb, the trig point comes into view, from which the views in all directions are excellent [3].

7. From the summit of Crugyn Ci, head off to the south to rejoin the bridleway, and then continue south westish down this path in the general direction of Penygarreg Farm. The path is easy to follow all the way down to the boundary of the farm, when you will encounter a wire fence. Cross the fence by the wooden stile provided, and continue downhill along the path to another wire fence and another stile. Cross this stile and continue downhill until you reach a grassy lane running left to right. Turn left (south eastish) and proceed down the lane past Penygarreg Farm, passing through a couple of gates and continuing along the farm lane before turning sharp right to cross Nant y Blymbren. Pass a black house on the left, and you will come to a junction of paths at GR 917 674 where you need to turn right, heading west once again. This is now part of the Elan Valley Trail (which leads from the Elan Valley Visitor's Centre to Craig Goch Reservoir). Continue to the Penygarreg Dam (at GR 912 675).

8. On reaching the gate above Penygarreg Dam, it is worthwhile taking a short detour to the left to gain a spectacular view of the water cascading over the top of the dam [4] into the entrance to Carreg-Ddu Reservoir. Pass through the main gate, then turn back on yourself to pass through the smaller gate on the left. There are now some wooden steps on the right leading down to the top of the dam. Having viewed the dam, return up to the main Elan Valley Trail bridleway, and continue along this path. After about 250m, the path diverges. Take the left fork through a wooden gate for about 2.5 km along the side of Penygarreg Reservoir to the start point at Craig Goch Dam.

Facilities:

The Elan Valley, and the town of Rhayader itself, are well supplied with places to stay and to eat and drink. The Tourist Information Centre in Rhayader should be able to supply up-to-date information regarding the availability of local accommodation. There is also a Visitor Centre in the Elan Valley (on the B4518 between the town and the start of the walk - this is easier to visit on walk 9) run by Dŵr Cymru (Welsh Water), which contains a cafe, gift shop, and various exhibits. An extension to the Centre was opened in May 1997 by the botanist David Bellamy. At the start of the walk at Craig Goch Dam, there are public conveniences, picnic tables, and tourist information.

Safety Notes:

Most of this walk follows well-defined paths. Should any problem arise prior to Esgair Perfedd, it is probably easiest simply to retrace your steps. Likewise, if any problem should arise from Crugyn Ci onwards it would probably be easiest to follow the well-defined paths down towards Penygarreg Farm. The only points where following the paths may be a problem in mist are around the uplands of Esgair Perfedd and north east of Crugyn Ci, where the paths are a little indistinct in places. If you become stranded in mist on Esgair Perfedd and lose the path, the best plan would be to bear north east - sooner or later you must hit the road, when turning right (south of east) will take you down into Rhayader. Similarly, if you lose your bearings north east of Crugyn Ci, heading due north will again bring you to the road (though be wary of blundering into the stream that you had to cross earlier).

Elan Valley Visitor Centre - Cnwch

OS Maps: 1:50 000 Landranger 147 (Elan Valley & Builth Wells);
                1:25 000 Pathfinder 969 (SN 86/96: Rhayader).
Start: Elan Valley Visitor Centre (GR 928 646)
Access: From Rhayader town centre, follow the B4518 (signed
                for the Elan Valley) to the Visitor Centre, which is
                signposted on the left hand side.
Parking: Car park at the Visitor Centre (£1 fee).
Grade: Easy to moderate - involves about 200m of ascent
                (rising to about 250m if you opt for the diversion into
                Cnwch Nature Trail). Although quite short, this walk
                affords numerous opportunities to take detours to gain a
                real flavour of the nature of the Elan Valley. Walking
                boots strongly recommended - there are some sections
                that may be slippery when wet.

*A fairly short walk, concentrating on the dams of the Elan Valley, with
a twist in the tail of the history of the dams. It is also possible to
combine this walk with a visit to the Elan Valley Visitor Centre and
the Cnwch Wood Nature Trail.*

Points of Interest:

1. Elan Valley Visitor Centre. The Elan Valley Visitor Centre contains
a cafe, public conveniences, gift shop, and various exhibits detailing
the local wildlife and the complexities of the Elan Valley water
management scheme. It is possible to obtain fishing permits here for
the reservoirs in the valley, which are stocked with brown trout. For
the walker, packed lunches can be obtained from the cafe, and books
and leaflets can be bought from the shop and information desk
detailing many walks in the area of the Centre. Most are very short, of
about a mile or so, but the Elan Valley Trail stretches for five miles
(eight kilometres) from the Visitor Centre to Penygarreg Dam. An

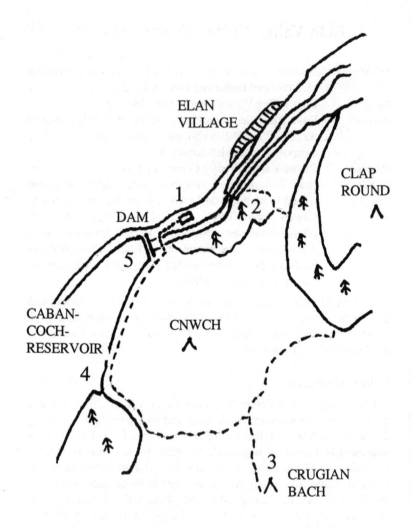

ELAN VILLAGE

CLAP ROUND

1

DAM

2

5

CABAN-
COCH-
RESERVOIR

CNWCH

4

3

CRUGIAN
BACH

extension to the Visitor's Centre was opened in May 1997 by the botanist David Bellamy. Be warned, however, that the gift and book shop does not accept any credit or debit cards (cash or cheque only) and at time of writing has no plans to do so.

2. Cnwch Wood Nature Trail. This delightful trail follows a well-managed path through the southern half of Cnwch Wood, which was designated a Site of Special Scientific Interest in 1965. Consisting mostly of various species of oak, the trail is rich in woodland fauna and flora, though is perhaps most interesting for the rich variety of bird life deliberately attracted to the area by the use of nesting boxes. It may be possible here to see redstarts, flycatchers, nuthatches and owls. Much natural history information is provided for the walker via the use of information panels along the route, of which there are no less than ten. Although a diversion along this trail would add a little distance to the walk, it is strongly recommended.

3. Crugian Bach. At about 450m above sea level, Crugian Bach does not present us with a particularly spectacular high point or summit, but it does provide some great views in all directions, and if it is rather breezy (which is not unusual around here!) it should be possible to find a place among the crags to eat your sandwiches with a certain degree of shelter. The area of Crugian Bach contains many hillocks, and it is necessary to nip from hillock to hillock to gain the best vantage point for each direction. This is one of those places whose mood is dictated by the weather. On a clear, sunny day it is positively cheerful here, but on a dull day the area radiates a bleakness that is almost malevolent. When dark clouds threaten, Allt Goch to the east broods menacingly, while the cairn on Cnwch to the north west almost appears a harbinger of doom. Yet, when the clouds disperse and the sun shines, the whole area lights up to provide the perfect picnic spot. About six or so miles away to the south west, clear weather would allow you to see the twin cairns of Drygarn Fawr, which at 645m above sea level is the highest point in the area.

4. Nant y Gro Dam. A small coffer dam designed originally to provide a water supply and hydroelectric power to the Elan Village (which itself was built to house the workers on the Elan Valley water scheme at the end of the Victorian era), the Nant y Gro Dam is no more, and

its ruins remind us of perhaps one of the strangest episodes in the history of the Elan Valley. The peaceful surroundings of hills, woodland and expanses of water that make up the valley may seem an unlikely place to become a top secret centre for the development of experimental forms of warfare, but in 1943 that was exactly what happened, and the valley was to play an important part in the planning of one of the most well-known episodes of World War II. It so happened that Nant y Gro Dam was of a similar design to the dams of the Ruhr Valley in Germany, which were the target of the famous Dambuster raid, and it was here that Barnes Wallace collected vital information for the development of the unique bouncing bomb that was used to such dramatic effect in that raid. The dam, of course, did not survive the experiments, and today only its ruins remain. Across the Caban-coch Reservoir, you may be able to see the Foel Tower, a deceptively complicated device that ensures that the water supply from the Elan Valley to Birmingham can be transported solely by the force of gravity by providing a sufficiently elevated outlet to the filter beds. Across the reservoir at this point you can also see what appears to be a road bridge. However, under the bridge is the submerged Garreg Ddu Dam, the top of which is usually about 12m below the waterline. This dam also plays a vital part in ensuring that the Foel Tower outlet is provided with water at all times. Better views of these structures can be had from the descent down from Crugian Bach.

5. Caban Coch Dam. The dam is 186m long, 38m thick at its base, and rises some 37m above the river bed, allowing the reservoir a capacity of about eight thousand million gallons over an area of 500 acres. It was built as part of the Elan Valley scheme of reservoirs at the end of the Victorian era, and opened on July 21st 1904 by King Edward VII. See the notes attached to walk 8 for more information concerning the dams of the Elan Valley.

Walk Directions:

1. From the car park at the Visitor Centre [1], walk back north east in the direction of the road to the Bailey Bridge that crosses the Elan. Cross the bridge and proceed to the wooden gate, then our main route heads off just east of north onto a waymarked footpath through the

north end of Cnwch Wood. (There is a possible diversion here, however, which would allow you to visit the Cnwch Wood Nature Trail [2] adding about 1.5 mls or 2.5 km to your walk; to do so, take the more obvious path south west, then follow the obvious zig zag path uphill through the wood to the end of the trail, before retracing your steps back to our main route.) To continue along our main route, turn left at the gate and follow the footpath over a stile, tending uphill along a wire fence. Arriving at a junction of paths, keep left and proceed to a stream. There are stepping stones here but they can be slippery. The path continues uphill fairly obviously to a grassy track near the road. Turn right onto this grassy track (following a line of telegraph poles) and continue uphill to the country lane at GR 934 646.

2. Turn right onto the lane, and follow this south, then south east for nearly 1 km (just over half a mile) over a cattle grid to a junction with a smaller lane on the right (at GR 937 639). Turn right here, then after about 75m turn right again, through a metal gate, to head uphill roughly west, then south west, along a narrow metalled road to a gate at the edge of woodland (at GR 931 633). Pass through the gate and onto open moorland.

3. Continue forward for about 25m to a junction of tracks. To the left a footpath heads off south east along the edge of the forestry and to the right the main bridleway heads off roughly south west towards Ty'n-y-Pant, but there is also a smaller path leading off south almost straight ahead. Take this smaller track south towards the crags of Crugian Bach, passing two rather inconspicuous cairns (presumably of Bronze Age origin) on the left. The crags and hillocks of Crugian Bach [3] do not represent the highest point in the area, but they afford a fine view in all directions.

4. From Crugian Bach, you need to rejoin the main track leading towards Ty'n-y-pant. The easiest way to do this is to retrace your steps to the gate at GR 931 633. However, the going is not too difficult here and you can save a little distance by striking off between north and north west to rejoin the obvious main track somewhere to the east of the ruined farmhouse of Ty'n-y-pant. In clear weather the best routes will be obvious, and you can use sheeptracks to make the going over

97

the heather and tussocks easier. In mist, care should be taken here - you should tend more north than north west and take it easy to avoid turning an ankle or tripping over. Either way, you want to arrive at the junction of paths at GR 929 632, where a bridleway is signposted left towards the south west and a footpath is signposted to the right almost due west. Take the footpath west, passing immediately north of Ty'n-y-pant, then continue to head towards the woodlands in front of you, tending very steeply down north east to follow the line of the forestry down to Caban-coch Reservoir at GR 922 636. Here is the ruin of Nant y Glo Dam [4].

5. Follow the waymarked path along the bank of Caban-coch Reservoir east of north towards Caban-coch Dam [5]. Just beyond the old stone viewing platform at the top of the dam, a stile on the left leads to a path descending steeply down to a footbridge across the Elan. Initially here there are some crumbling stone steps requiring care, then newer wooden steps make the going easier. Cross the footbridge, pass round the building and head back north of east back to the start point at the Visitor Centre.

Facilities:

The Elan Valley, and the town of Rhayader itself, are well supplied with places to stay and to eat and drink. The Tourist Information Centre in Rhayader should be able to supply up-to-date information regarding the availability of local accommodation. The Elan Valley Visitor Centre also contains many facilities (see above).

Safety Notes:

Virtually the entire walk follows well-defined paths, and therefore there should be no problem with navigation even in the worst weather. About the only place that mist could cause problems would be around Crugian Bach. If you lose you bearings here, simply head slightly west of north. Eventually you must hit the main bridlepath leading to Ty'n-y-pant. Alternatively, you could head due west, in which case sooner or later you must hit either Caban-coch Reservoir, or (more likely) the forestry on its eastern bank. Then simply follow the line of forestry northish to the path along the bank of the reservoir. If you head west, though, great care must be taken over the moorland - there are many tussocks and rocks to trip the unwary, and some sections are very steep.

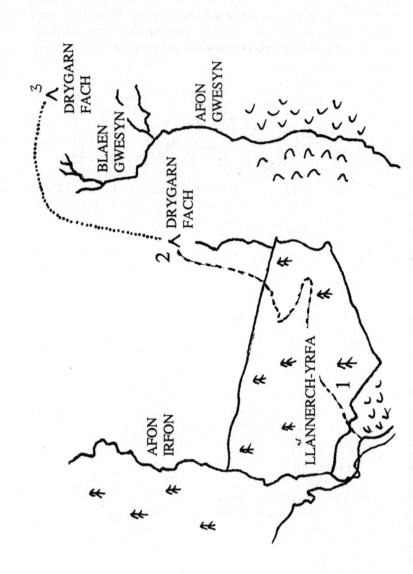

100

Llannerch-yrfa - Drygarn Fach
(Possible extension to Drygarn Fawr)

OS Maps:	1:50 000 Landranger 147 (Elan Valley & Builth Wells area); 1:25 000 Pathfinder 991 (SN 85/95: Beulah & Abergwesyn).
Start:	Bridge over the Irfon at GR 836 555.
Access:	From the A483 at Llanwrtyd Wells, take the turning signposted for Abergwesyn at the crossroads in the middle of the town. Continue along this road to Abergwesyn, then turn left onto a narrow country lane signposted for Llyn Brianne. The start point for the walk is a couple of miles down this road. (IMPORTANT: See Safety Notes below).
Parking:	There is room for a car or two at the side of the road just before the Landrover track leading into the forest. Make sure that enough room is left to allow this area to be used as a passing place.
Grade:	Moderate - involves about 260m ascent in total. Forest tracks, bridleways and open countryside. Walking boots essential - can be extremely boggy in places. This walk should not be attempted in mist (see Safety Notes below). If the extension to Drygarn Fawr is attempted, the walk may be regarded as strenuous (expanding to at least 7 mls/11 km with a total ascent of about 430m). The extended walk should only be attempted in fine, clear weather.

A deceptive walk. Though not long, it crosses difficult ground, especially after wet weather, and will give the walker a taste of the unique character of the bleak Cwmdeuddwr Hills. It includes a sight of the most spectacular cairns in Wales on Drygarn Fawr, and although an extension to the summit of Drygarn Fawr is possible it should only be attempted by those confident with map and compass in fine weather.

Points of Interest:

1. Llannerch-yrfa. Afforestation is a phenomenon widely condemned by the walking fraternity, and a glance at this general area on the 1:50 000 map will show you why. Huge dollops of land to the west and south are covered with conifers, and much walking country is rendered impassable, or at least joyless, to the walker. Having said that, though, the Llannerch-yrfa area of the forest is not too extensive, and is very easy to navigate. There are also numerous mini-waterfalls that can be enjoyed along the path, though these may be dry after prolonged periods of fine weather. There is little notable about Llannerch-yrfa itself - if you've seen one conifer forest you've seen the lot - but to the east of the forest there is a vast tract of land around Esgair Irfon and Afon Gwesyn that has been designated as a nature reserve. The Esgair Irfon Nature Reserve is looked after by the Brecknock Wildlife Trust, and is reputedly home to cliff nesting birds. However, the more extensive area leading north up Cwm Gwesyn across Abergwesyn Common and far as, and including, Drygarn Fawr itself, is controlled by the National Trust, and since grazing is limited around these areas you may be fortunate enough to come across such exotica as bilberry, crowberry and even cowberry (...no, I'd never heard of it either).

2. Drygarn Fach. By the time you reach Drygarn Fach, the nature of the Cwmdeuddwr hills should now be fairly clear. For Cwmdeuddwr is very different to the other mountain groups of Central Wales. Here there are no dramatic peaks and few spectacular valleys. In truth, this is really an area of high moorland where vast tracts of empty land undulate gently above 500m or so, and peaty bog is the rule rather than the exception. Indeed, the great problem of Cwmdeuddwr for the walker is the nature of the ground. A glance at the map suggests a multitude of walks around here: Drygarn Fawr, Gorllwyn, Drum yr Eira - all look ripe for visiting. Yet once you get out there you find that the boggy, tussocky ground can give horrendously difficult walking even in the drier times of high summer. For this reason, I have

102

restricted the walking of Cwmdeuddwr covered in this book, although the possible extension to Drygarn Fawr suggested below will demonstrate the nature of Cwmdeuddwr better than a thousand words on a page. For my money, Cwmdeuddwr is very much like the interior bogland of Dartmoor, only without the proliferation of tors. Cwmdeuddwr, though, is not without its charm, and although its high points might be thought to be rather bleak, after the fashion of Great Rhos in the Radnor Forest, it somehow manages to convey a sense of wilderness and solitude that even Great Rhos cannot manage. I have seen Cwmdeuddwr described a thousand different ways: as an empty wasteland, as a gently undulating sea, or as the last great wilderness in Wales. I have even seen Cwmdeuddwr described as dangerous, though it is only so to the reckless. Yet all agree that Cwmdeuddwr is *different*, and it is rarely visited. This is a shame, because to ignore Cwmdeuddwr is to ignore one of Central Wales more unusual facets. Drygarn Fach itself, to be honest, is not much to write home about. There is no obvious summit, as such, and it does not so much rise majestically above the high moorland as bubble up from it gently. But it does give a great feel for the area, and probably provides the best local viewpoint short of Drygarn Fawr itself. With the exception of those two preposterous cairns atop big brother Drygarn Fawr, all the drama is in the distance, particularly to the south, where on a fine day you may be able to make out the majesty of all the high ridges of the Brecon Beacons National Park, from the Black Mountains to your left to Mynydd Du on the right. Closer by, though, in pretty much all directions, Cwmdeuddwr simply ripples remorselessly in its silent, boggy way, though to the north you should be able to see a small cairn marking the way north to Drum yr Eira. It is not difficult to see why navigation here is difficult in mist - there is little to navigate by! To be out here without a map and compass would be folly indeed.

3. Drygarn Fawr. Even viewed from Drygarn Fach, the twin beehive cairns atop Drygarn Fawr are spectacular. Over 3m in height, these cairns were originally Bronze Age in origin, though their current appearance is relatively modern. There were originally three cairns here - hence the name of Drygarn which means "three cairns" - and the summit cairn was utilised in the nineteenth century as a triangulation

point by the Ordinance Survey. The two surviving cairns, however, were rebuilt in 1894 to their current appearance by the Birmingham City Corporation responsible for the Elan Valley water management scheme, as they mark the boundary of the water catchment area for the Elan Valley reservoirs. It is useful to the walker that these cairns are so large; since Cwmdeuddwr in general is so devoid of shelter it is pleasant to be able to stand or sit in the lee of one of the cairns to eat your sandwiches. Drygarn Fawr also boasts a modern trig point - the summit is 645m above sea level and it represents the high point of the Cwmdeuddwr hills. The walk to Drygarn Fawr from Drygarn Fach is difficult, though if you can make it the view is worthwhile. As from Drygarn Fach, the south is dominated by the massif of the Brecon Beacons National Park, though now the summit cairns of Gorllwyn (Cwmdeuddwr's second highest point) are visible to the east. On a fine day, you should be able to make out Pumlumon to the north west, and with a bit of luck you should be able to make out Cadair Idris sneakily poking its nose out from behind Pumlumon.

Walk Directions:

1. From the start point, head north east up the semi-metalled Landrover track into the forest. Although the track proceeds relentlessly uphill, the gradient is not too steep and the going here is very easy. You will soon come to a gate. Pass through this, and continue along the track deep into the forest of Llannerch-yrfa [1].

2. After almost a mile, the track hairpins back to the left. Continue left to follow it, then after a few hundred metres you will come to a junction. The left fork continues along more or less flat. However, you want to take the right fork, which hairpins round to the right uphill. Immediately after this bend you will see a curious crescent-shaped gouge in the rock on the left hand side of the track. This marks the point where you want to leave the main track (which continues on east). To the right of the crescent-shaped gouge is a large conifer (one of many!) around which is a very muddy path leading to an even muddier path heading just south of north east through the trees. The path is quite obvious, though as this area is sheltered from the sun it is likely to be squlechy going even in high summer. The path continues

for about 250m or so, and leads you to the edge of the forest at GR 848 564. Here there is a gate leading to the open countryside.

3. Pass through the gate. The path, marked as a bridleway on the 1:25 000 map, is quite obvious, leading north east in the general direction of Drygarn Fach. In fact, this bridleway passes to the south of Drygarn Fach, and although it appears to offer the easiest walking this appearance is deceptive, as after about 500m or so you will arrive at Nant Fedw and you will, at least after wet weather, find it very difficult to cross without getting your feet wet. Rather, from the gate, it is much easier to make a beeline for the highest visible point of Drygarn Fach, which is just east of north. Freelance uphill, and you will soon find two hillocks - which are not really high or dramatic enough to describe as summits - appearing in front of you. The one to the left is wide and gentle, while the one to the right is narrower and has a characteristic snub-nosed appearance. The easiest way up is to make for the saddle between them, before turning again to the north east towards the snub-nosed hillock. This now marks what is more or less the summit of Drygarn Fach [2], though you may want to wander around a bit to get the best viewpoints of Drygarn Fawr [3] to the north east and the Brecon Beacons far away to the south.

3a. POSSIBLE EXTENSION TO DRYGARN FAWR. If the weather is iffy, or if you have got wet attaining the summit of Drygarn Fach on cold weather, do not attempt this extension. However, if you are dry, the weather is fine, and you have plenty of daylight time in hand, the walk to Drygarn Fawr will provide a mountain adventure to be remembered. This is one of those wilderness walks where paths do not lie conveniently to hand, and the walker must rely on his or her own abilities with map and compass to chart a route across open country. The obvious route from Drygarn Fach to Drygan Fawr is more or less direct. After all, on the map there appears to be a bridleway leading from the south side of Drygarn Fach almost right past Drygarn Fawr. This, however is an illusion. The bridleway, which led from the forest to the south side of Drygarn Fach, peters out very quickly, and the bridleway beyond this point effectively does not exist on the ground (avoid the temptation to follow horse tracks on the assumption that they must mark the bridleway - there are often some wild ponies grazing in this area whose tracks could lead you a merry dance!). Even worse, the terrain it appears to cross is awful - it is extremely boggy and it consists almost entirely of peat hags and tussocks. Wet feet are a certainty and a twisted ankle is an uncomfortable possibility. As suggested above, anyone familiar with the terrain of the interior of Dartmoor will be familiar with the slow, foot-squelching, ankle-jarring and deeply tiring nature of the walking you can expect, and frankly it isn't worth the candle. In fact, although most of the terrain around here is less than easy to walk, there is a route that will take you away from the worst of it. The way to go from Drygarn Fach is north - heading to the visible cairn in the distance towards the upland plateau of Drum yr Eira, before bearing off east towards Drygarn Fawr, trying to avoid the worst of the bog around Blaen Gwesyn. The river is not so much of a problem here, but the bog-hopping can be tiresome. Either way, arrival at the summit of Drygarn Fawr will seem like - and is - an achievement. The best way to return to Drygarn Fach is via the way you came - it may be difficult and tiring but at least you know it is possible.

4. From Drygarn Fach, retrace your steps to the forest, and thence back to the start point. Finding the grassy path back can be a bit of a chore, but if you can find it you will discover the going much easier. As a rule of thumb, I usually think that the path is just a little bit further downhill than I remembered it. I usually find it then!

Facilities:

Very little is available locally - the nearest town of appreciable size is Llanwrtyd Wells, where shops, pubs and bed and breakfast facilities can be found. The excellent Tourist Information Centre in Llanwrtyd Wells will be able to help you with accommodation in the area.

Safety Notes:

Unusually, the first safety point for this walk concerns events before you even arrive at the start point. The country lane leading along the Irfon Valley from Abergwesyn towards the start point is gorgeously picturesque but potentially hazardous, especially after bad weather.

The main problem is that the valley falls away steeply down the left hand side, and there is no fence bordering the road. Extreme care should be taken, therefore, along this road, which can be very wet indeed after rain, as water from the massif to the right drains down onto and across the road and into the valley. There are also many twists and turns, which can arrive quite unexpectedly. Having said that, however, so long as the weather hasn't been too bad, a careful driver should have no problem.

Although the initial forest walk through Llannerch-yrfa suggests that navigation for this walk should be a piece of cake, this easy start flatters to deceive. Once you emerge into open countryside north of the forest, navigation can quickly become a nightmare in mist. The very nature, and perhaps the attraction, of the Cwmdeuddwr area is that it is open and curiously featureless, and although you will, in fine weather, be presented with some pretty unmistakable markers (such as the cairns atop Drygarn Fawr and the edge of the forest of Llannerch-yrfa), you will find that the disappearance of these markers in mist means that you have to rely solely on your compass. It is very strongly recommended, therefore, that if mist is apparent or expected, you should probably not attempt this walk (and you should certainly not attempt the extension). If you are caught in mist, however, in the vicinity of Drygarn Fach north of the forest, the best plan is to set your compass for south west and to head for the northern boundary of the forest. Take care not to stray too much to the west, where you may end up around the crags surrounding Nant y Rhos; if anything, tend slightly south of south west until you hit the forest. when it simply becomes a matter of locating the gate denoting the way home. If you have attempted the extension to Drygarn Fawr, and then you get caught in mist, this is where the fun really starts. Unfortunately, because of the nature of the terrain between Drygarn Fach and Drygarn Fawr, and the interruption of the Gwesyn, there is no good way of setting a single compass bearing that will get you to a convenient collecting point on the way home. The best plan is to set your compass to the west, and proceed in this direction until you reach the flattish plateau between Drygarn Fach and Drum yr Eira. Then set the compass south towards Drygarn Fach, from which you can proceed as above.

Bryn Garw

OS Maps:	1:50 000 Landranger 135 (Aberystwyth & surrounding area); 1:25 000 Pathfinder 947 (SN 67/77: Devil's Bridge & Llanilar).
Start:	Car park at the George III Jubilee Arch (GR 766 756).
Access:	From Ponterwyd on the A44 Aberystwyth-Llangurig road, turn south onto the A4120 for Devil's Bridge. At Devil's Bridge, take the B4574 signposted for Cwmystwyth. This road passes directly under the George III Jubilee Arch, and the car park is immediately adjacent.
Parking:	Free car park.
Grade:	Moderate - involves about 250m ascent in total. Almost all forest tracks. Walking boots probably not essential, but desirable in bad weather.

A fairly straightforward walk along a forest trail leading to some majestic viewpoints of the major Cwmdeuddwr hills to the south and Pumlumon to the north. Depending on the current fencing policy of the local landowners, the summit of Bryn Garw may not be accessible.

Points of Interest:

1. George III Jubilee Arch. This arch was erected by Thomas Johnes of Hafod in 1810 to mark the golden jubilee of the accession of George III, and was renovated and strengthened in 1964 in a joint venture between the Forestry Commission, Cardiganshire County Council and the Cardiganshire Antiquarian Society. Johnes was also responsible for much of the re-afforestation of the area between 1780 and 1813, having noted that much of the ancient forestry around here had been damaged or destroyed by the lead mining and smelting activity that had been so important to the local economy. The forestry here is now carefully managed by the Forestry Commission, who have

also provided a number of facilities for walkers, including the car park and public conveniences. Tourist information is provided at the car park, and there are also three short waymarked forestry trails (0.5 miles, 1 mile, and 1.5 miles in length) in the area. It is stated that trail guides are available from an honesty box, although on my last visit there was no sign of this (this was, however, well out of the main tourist season).

2. Golygfan Viewpoint. Situated above Craig y Ceffyl, this viewpoint affords a spectacular view across the Rhuddnant Valley. Deep down in the valley below you will see Nant Rhuddnant, with a forest road shadowing it from left to right, and you will also see the menacing crags of Craig Dolwen on the far side of the nant, beyond which the forest continues for some distance to the tops of Pen Dihewyd and Banc Nantycreuau. It is to the far horizon, however, that the gaze is irresistibly drawn, and you may be able to see the high tops of the Pumlumon hills to the north with their summit cairns. You should also be able to see a windfarm at about 295 degrees. Even if the summit of Bryn Garw is not attainable (see below), this panorama provides a fitting climax to the walk.

3. Bryn Garw. Marked as Pen y Garn on the most up-to-date OS maps, Bryn Garw is not a particularly impressive summit, though at 610m above sea level it marks the third highest top in the Cwmdeuddwr area. Actually, Bryn Garw has something of a semi-detached feel as far as Cwmdeuddwr is concerned; it is well to the north west of the main peaks, and the nature of the ground is quite different to the horrible boggy, tussocky land around Gorllwyn and Drygarn Fawr. An attempt at the summit is probably worthwhile for peak-bagging purposes, but to be fair the views described above from the forest trail are as good as anything you will see from Bryn Garw, and, as stated below, the summit may be inaccessible as a consequence of fences erected by farmers.

Walk Directions:

1. From the car park, take the main track into the forest, past the "no entry to vehicles" sign, and you will soon come to a crossroads.

Continue on uphill roughly north east, slightly to the right. The track bends round further to the right, and you will pass a footpath off to the left. Keep on the main track, though, and proceed to the area marked on the map as Coed y Cŵn. Here there is a bit of a clearing to the right, and you can gain a first glimpse of the Cwmdeuddwr hills in the distance to the south and south east.

2. Continue on along the main track to Coed y Ceuleth, where you will see obvious footpaths leading off left and right. Stick, however, to the main track which bends round to the left east of Truman, and leads to a junction with another track to the left. Stick to the main track again, however, and soon you will emerge in a cleared part of the forest. Here, on the right, a large area of tall trees has been cut down and replanted with much smaller trees, allowing you a cracking view to the south of the Cwmdeuddwr hills - you may be able to make out both Drygarn Fawr and Gorllwyn.

3. The main track now continues sweeping round to the right, and then to the left as it steers its way around a densely planted area - you can see the track here for some way ahead. Continue on up, ignoring another track leading sharpish right, and on to another clearing where there is a peculiar lay-by arrangement with a track leading off south, to the right, into the forest. Ignore these, however, and just keep on the main track - you are now approaching the Craig y Ceffyl area, and soon you will reach the edge of the forestry. First, however, you will come to the Golygfan viewpoint [2], before you emerge into open country with Bryn Garw rising to your right [3].

4. Most walking guides suggest that you now head uphill to the right for the final pull up to the summit of Bryn Garw. It used to be possible to do this with ease, but on my last visit the whole area was criss crossed with electrified wire fencing and the ascent was not possible. Still, despite this disappointment, it must be acknowledged that the views that can be had from Bryn Garw are no better than those from Golygfan and the east side of Truman, which you will be able to enjoy once again on the return to the car park. The return route is simply a matter of re-tracing your steps through the forest.

Facilities:

There is a picnic site and public conveniences at the start point (though the latter often seem to be locked out of the summer holiday season). The nearest main centre is Devil's Bridge, which itself contains some nice walking country, though it is all a bit commercialised and tourist-oriented, especially in the summer. Camping and hotel accommodation are also available near here. There are numerous things to see and experience, however, around Devil's Bridge, including the waterfalls at the Devil's Punchbowl, the terminus of the Vale of Rheidol narrow gauge railway, which runs to Aberystwyth, and, of course, the bridge itself - or rather bridges, for there are three. The famous legend has it that the original bridge here was built by the Devil himself. Apparently Old Nick's idea was that the first living thing to cross the bridge would belong to him, and having built the bridge, he lay in wait. A local woman by the name of Megan Llandunach had lost a cow, and she spied it across the gorge. The only way across, of course, was via the Devil's Bridge, and Old Nick invited her across. Megan was wise to his idea, however, and before she crossed she threw a crust across the bridge for her hungry dog to chase and eat. Since her dog was the first living thing to cross the bridge, she could then cross in safety and retrieve her cow (although I can imagine that the dog wasn't entirely happy about this).

Safety Notes:

Since virtually the whole walk is along unmistakable forest tracks, navigation for this walk is a doddle. However, should you get stuck in mist while making an attempt on the summit of Bryn Garw, then heading north west will bring you back to the forest track. Probably the only safety note worth making is a warning about logging activity. You may well come across workmen engaged in cutting down trees, and you will need to be very careful when approaching such work. Falling trees and whirring chainsaws can be bad for your health.

Llanwrtyd Wells - Garn Dwad

OS Maps:	1:50000 Landranger 147 (Elan Valley & Builth Wells area); 1:25000 Pathfinder 1014 (SN 84/94: Llanwrtyd Wells).
Start:	Neuadd Arms Hotel, Llanwrtyd Wells
Access:	The start point is situated on the A470 between Llandovery and Builth Wells. Alternatively, Llanwrtyd lies on the Heart of Wales railway line, and is easily accessed via Shrewsbury or Swansea.
Parking:	There is a car park at the Neuadd Arms Hotel. Alternatively, there is plentiful parking available around Llanwrtyd Wells.
Grade:	Moderate - involves about 250m ascent in total. Bridleways and open countryside. Walking boots recommended.

A glorious country hike around one of the most popular walking areas in Central Wales. Llanwrtyd Wells is oozing with history, and its accompanying hills afford some fine views of the area.

Points of Interest:

1. Llanwrtyd Wells. It is a proud boast locally that Llanwrtyd Wells is in the Guinness Book of Records as being officially the smallest town in Britain, with a stable population of approximately five hundred. I do not know precisely how a small town is differentiated from a large village - presumably it has something to do with having won borough status at some time in the past - but Llanwrtyd Wells certainly has the confident air of a town, albeit a tiny one. It was not ever thus, however. Originally a small hamlet, there were two events which signalled the development of the modern town. The first was the discovery of natural springs (see the notes concerning the Dôl-y-Coed Hotel, below), which provided a magnet for visitors for the first time.

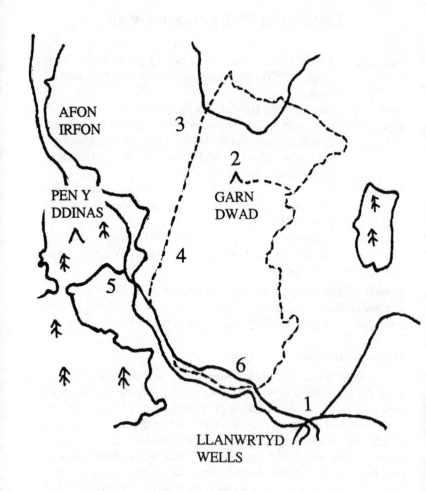

AFON
IRFON

PEN Y
DDINAS

3

2
GARN
DWAD

4

5

6

1

LLANWRTYD
WELLS

The second was the development of the railways (Llanwrtyd Wells still has its own station on the Heart of Wales line between Shrewsbury and Swansea), which at last made transport to Llanwrtyd Wells easy for the masses, and the town transformed into a centre for holidaying. These days, the locals manage rather well to walk a tightrope between the promotion of the town as a tourist centre and the tendency to overdo things and spoil the atmosphere of the place. It is true that some of the more tourist-orientated activities are of doubtful historical relevance (such as the world bog-snorkelling championships which take place here during the summer), but for the most part Llanwrtyd Wells makes the most of its history without detracting from the charm and beauty of the area.

* * *

The Drovers

These days, Llanwrtyd Wells is a major centre for those of us who enjoy long distance walking as a recreational activity, but in former times it was a major centre for walking of a quite different nature. For Llanwrtyd Wells was an important stopping point for the drovers, a connection that is remembered to this day as an important feature of it's history.

The origins of droving are pretty clear. Until the time of the industrial revolution, one's livelihood, as likely as not, was derived from agriculture, and as society became more and more sophisticated, the necessity to find a market for the livestock one reared would become more and more pressing. Often, the local market was not capable of sustaining the degree of economic activity necessary to maintain the families of the farmers, and so markets further afield had to be explored and utilised. To the farmers of all parts of Wales, but of Central Wales in particular, this essentially meant taking their cattle to England to be sold. For many centuries, from the invasion of the Normans to the industrial revolution, the primary income for many cattle farmers was derived from the sale of their herds in the great English markets, such as that at Hereford, and this, of course, meant the mass movement of herds across Wales to England.

This was no easy matter. Even today, the road network between the western parts of Central Wales and England is not exactly highly developed, but prior to the twentieth century it would have been far more difficult. Proper roads would have been few and far between, and the metalled surfaces of the modern era would not have existed. The drovers' routes would essentially have had to have evolved across country, and a slow, messy business it would have been. The modern walker will be familiar with the churned up footpath or bridleway, muddy and squelchy from use by walking boots and shoed hooves when there has been a little rain, or hard and rutted in high summer when the mud has had time to bake. Imagine how much worse such country routes must have been for the drovers, when, in one year alone, up to thirty thousand head of cattle may have been moved along them, rain or shine, with their associated herdsmen and their ponies - and this would not have included the regular, everyday traffic. Neither would the mud and muck have been the only hazard. These were lawless times, and footpads and bandits would prey upon hapless travellers out in the wilds and far from help. The drovers may well have been expected to be carrying money with them for their long journey (and even more, they would hope, on the way back), and so they would have to be ready to defend themselves against such attack. Often, other travellers, unconnected with the drove, would accompany them on their way for the protection they might afford. It might also be remembered that wolves only became extinct in these islands relatively recently. This was obviously no walk in the park!

At least the drovers' skill was rewarded. Many drovers could expect to earn more than the average agriculturally-related wage of the day, and by Elizabethan times drovers had to be licensed to work at their craft. In later years, as commerce became more and more important, the senior drovers would also undertake financial dealings in England on behalf of their masters. In days when communication over distances was vastly more difficult than it is today, the drovers were also often bearers of news of those strange, far off places in England, and they would sometimes bring back with them goods, from Europe or the East, that may have been everyday things to the well heeled of the English gentry and middle classes, but which must have seemed exotic indeed in rural Central Wales.

The main drovers' routes in the area run roughly east from Abergwesyn. Initially, Llanwrtyd Wells was by-passed, as the drovers would drive their cattle east from Abergwesyn to Beulah, a few miles north of Llanwrtyd Wells along the A483, before continuing east to Builth Wells and thence towards the border via Kington. However, the building of the railways made life rather easier for the drovers, who could now head south from Abergwesyn, following the course of the Irfon, to Llanwrtyd Wells. Here, cattle could be herded onto trains heading east to Reading. This route is now, of course, metalled, and forms the minor road from Llanwrtyd Wells to Abergwesyn. The character of the route, however, is otherwise unspoilt, and the road provides perhaps one of the most magnificent scenic routes to be enjoyed from a motor car anywhere in the country.

These days, of course, there are no more drovers as such. The role of the drovers, and latterly of the railways too, has largely been taken over by lorries which can do the job rather more cheaply. Nevertheless, Llanwrtyd Wells is proud of its droving history, and the town is dotted with references to this aspect of its past. Indeed, each year there is a walking festival that takes place in the summer, known as the Drovers' Walk, starting from the square in the middle of the town and taking a different route around the glorious walking country surrounding it, from distances of about 10 km right up to adventurous mountain hikes of 40 km. A badge can be bought by everyone who takes part in the walk, attesting to the droving history of this fascinating town in the middle of some of Wales' most beautiful countryside. (The badge, along with many other walking trophies, can be seen in the Neuadd Arms Hotel).

* * *

2. Garn Dwad. It is a shame that the true summit of Garn Dwad is not attainable from this side, but the 440m spot height takes us to with a few metres of the very top, and the view is spectacular nevertheless. To the west lies Llyn Brianne and the Towy Forest, while to the north

lie the rolling hills of Cwmdeuddwr. The view to the south, of course, is dominated by the true summit of Garn Dwad, but to the east, if you have with you the 1:50 000 OS map, you can spend much time playing name the peak, although on most days you will actually be spending most of your time trying to keep the map from blowing away! It is a slight pity that you do not really get a good commanding view of Llanwrtyd from here, though from further down the eastern slope you can get the occasional glimpse of it snugly nestling in the valley away to the south. Also, on the southern slopes of Garn Dwad, there are a number of ancient cairns, presumably Bronze Age in origin.

3. Pen-y-Banc. The building below and to the right of the track here is Pen-y-banc, which was (and as far as I know still is) owned by the family of Sir Daniel Davies, who was, along with the far more famous Aneurin Bevan, one of the architects of the modern National Health Service.

4. Kilsby. This pretty little cottage, with attractive French-style wooden window shutters, set back a little from the country lane, is named after James Rhys Jones ("Kilsby"), a writer and poet, who once owned it.

5. St David's Church. This unprepossessing church stands on a site that has been regarded as holy for many hundreds of years. The Celtic cross inside the church suggests that the current building was predated by previous structures dating back as many as 1,400 years. The graves of a number of famous Welshmen are to be found here, including the composer John Thomas and the hymn-writer William Williams.

6. Dôl-y-Coed Hotel. It is this hotel that is essentially responsible for the "Wells" in Llanwrtyd Wells. In the eighteenth century, when medicine was not quite what it is today, there was something of a craze for sulphurous natural springs, whose waters were meant to carry healing properties and to promote general good health and well-being. In 1732, a historian named Theophilus Evans, author of the religious tract *Mirror of the First Ages*, who was suffering from scurvy at the time, claimed that the natural springs here conferred healing and good health, presumably because his scurvy cleared up after he had taken the waters. It is highly unlikely that the waters actually had anything to do with it - scurvy is caused by vitamin C deficiency and a few citrus

fruit or other vitamin C-rich foods would soon put the problem straight - but Evans seems to have been convinced that the waters were responsible for his recovery, and he was soon promoting the waters of the Stinking Well (Ffynnon Droellwyd) as a jolly good thing all round. Needless to say the idea soon took off, as it did in various other places in the area (including Llandrindod, Builth, and Llangammarch, hence their modern place names), and the future of Llanwrtyd in general, and the Dôl-y-Coed Hotel (originally a farmhouse built circa 1535) in particular, was assured, and other wells around the town, particularly at Henfron and Victoria (where the Victoria Wells Hotel still stands) also attracted many visitors. It is difficult now to believe that people used to drink this malodourous concoction, let alone think that it was actually doing them good. Thank goodness for modern medicine!

Walk Directions:

1. From the square in the middle of Llanwrtyd Wells, walk north of west up the country lane signposted for Abergwesyn (this is the old drovers' road). The great hill of Banc y Ddinas looms up on your left hand side. Carry on to the Dôl-y-Coed Hotel, which appears on the left hand side of the road. Opposite the hotel you will see a drive on the right, which is waymarked as a bridleway on the 1:25 000 OS map. Turn right up this drive, and soon you will come to a fork. The right-hand fork leads into some buildings, but we want the left-hand fork, which continues as the bridleway. The track is still semi-metalled and is easy walking, and soon Lofftwen Farm comes into view ahead.

2. Continue to the farm, which you will have to walk though (this is a right of way) ignoring any barking dogs that may greet you. Head up north from the farm for about 150m or so, to a junction of tracks. Here, a grassy track leads off west down to the Abergwesyn road, but we want to continue north east uphill along the main bridleway. After a couple of hundred metres or so, the path takes a ninety degree turn to the left, and then after another hundred or so metres it takes another ninety degree turn to the left up to the derelict farmhouse of Ffos-y-fign.

3. At the farmhouse, the path becomes narrower, and winds around to the right to a gate and a track leading from left to right. Turn right and

follow the track to another gate just ahead. Beyond this gate, the track continues very obviously across the next field to another gate. Pass through this gate, and continue north along the line of trees, keeping them to your immediate left. The views to the right here are splendid. To the north east is the rounded hill of Y Foel, while straight in front is the massif comprising the various tops of Pen y Garn-goch, Pen Dysgwylfa and Crugwydd. You are now on the eastern slopes of Garn Dwad.

4. At the end of the avenue of trees, there is a gate to the left, and the bridleway takes another ninety degree turn to the left. Pass through this gate, and continue along this green lane for a little over a hundred metres, before taking yet another ninety degree turn, this time to the right, to follow the bridleway more or less north to Geufron. Immediately beyond Geufron, the path diverges. The obvious driveway that serves Geufron veers downhill to the right. However, we need to keep left in a roughly north eastern direction to follow the bridleway towards Nant-gwyn. To do this, head slightly uphill and to the left, following the course of the wire fence. For its initial few metres, this does not look like a bridleway, but soon the path becomes much more obvious, bounded by wire fencing on both sides.

5. Continue to follow the obvious path, which initially bends round to the left, before bringing you to the bubbling stream of Nant Gwyn. Cross the nant, and follow the path forwards to a gate. Pass through the gate and continue roughly north east to the end of the field. Here there are two gates: to the right, there is a wide metal farm gate and to the left there is a narrower very rickety old wooden gate. Pass through the narrower left hand gate, beyond which there is a choice of routes. The marked bridleway continues roughly north east, following the boundary of the field, but there is also an obvious path leading off uphill to the left. Take this uphill path to the left, and make for the summit of Garn Dwad. The path is very obvious for most of the way. The easiest strategy is to make for the two crags on the hillside, each of which boasts a single tree. Then, from the more southerly of the two trees head off more or less west to the summit. This will actually take you to the 440m spot height, immediately to the east of a wire fence, which is not quite the summit. Unfortunately, the 446m spot height,

which is the true summit, is the other side of the wire fence and is not accessible from here. Still, the 440m top, which is crowned with a cairn, affords some great views [2].

6. From the 440m top, return to the trees which marked your route up, and then re-trace your steps downhill back to the main bridleway by the gates. From here, continue along the bridleway north east, and down to the forest road junction at GR 881 488. Turn left here, and follow the forest road north, then north west, following Nant Cerdin to the forest edge at GR 876 492. Cross the cattle grid and follow the road into the forest. After a few metres, take the smaller road off to the left, heading somewhat uphill and quickly winding round to the right. This continues uphill for a while, before bending round to the right and coming to a junction of bridleways.

7. At this junction, turn sharp left to follow the waymarked bridleway uphill, heading roughly south west. Follow this track to the edge of the forest and back into open country. Continue to follow this obvious track just west of south, passing Pen-y-banc [3] on the right and Kilsby [4] on the left, noting the majestic green dome of Pen y Ddinas to the right, and St David's Church [5] at its foot, until you reach the Abergwesyn road once more at GR 866 476. Bear left here, heading back towards Llanwrtyd Wells. After about half a kilometre, you will see a waymarked footpath on the right leading down to the banks of the Irfon. Take this path, and follow the river down to the rear of the Dôl-y-Coed Hotel [6] at GR 874 469. Rejoin the Abergwesyn road here, and proceed back into Llanwrtyd Wells.

Facilities:

Llanwrtyd Wells is well geared up for the tourist. There are shops and pubs locally, and the excellent Tourist Information Centre should be able to guide you as to the availability of accommodation. The only bank in Llanwrtyd Wells, a branch of Barclays, was recently the target of a successful campaign by the locals to ward off its closure. The Neuadd Arms Hotel, which together with the adjacent Red Kite Activity Centre forms a major focus for walking in the area, is open all day, and serves coffee in the morning. There are a number of permanent trails around the Llanwrtyd area, which have been produced under the auspices of the IVV (an international walking federation). This walk shadows one of the trails to a certain extent, but details of the full 10 km trail (and of the other three that exist at time of writing) are available either from the Neuadd Arms Hotel or from the Tourist Information Centre.

Safety Notes:

Navigation for this walk should provide few problems, as most of the way follows well defined bridleways and forest tracks. The only spot of open country is on the ascent to the summit of Garn Dwad. If you get stranded in mist here, the footpaths back to the main bridleway should be fairly obvious, or, if you have strayed from them, head roughly slightly south of east (watching for crags and steep slopes) and allow yourself to be guided back to the main bridleway by the wire fences that criss cross the area.

Mynydd yr Eithin - Whimble - Black Mixen

OS Maps: 1:50 000 Landranger 148 (Presteigne & Hay-on-Wye); 1:25 000 Pathfinders 970 (SO 06/16: Llandrindod Wells) & 971 (SO 26/36: Presteigne).

Start: New Radnor village centre (GR 213 609).

Access: New Radnor is situated on the B4372 just off the A44 between Kington and Llanfihangel-Nant-Melan.

Parking: It should be easy to park on the street at or near the start point. Note that while it may be tempting to drive up Mutton Dingle to find a parking place further up that will cut out some of the early climb, this temptation should be resisted - there is no good parking place higher up and you may inadvertently end up blocking access to the forest, which is continually required by Forestry Commission vehicles.

Grade: Moderate to Strenuous - involves about 390m of ascent. It is possible to cut out about 80m of ascent by missing out the ascent of Whimble (which would make the walk more moderate than strenuous). Walking boots essential - the bridleways soon take you out into wild mountain country and the high moorland can be quite boggy, particularly after wet weather.

A hefty walk out onto one of the two high moorland plateaux of the Radnor Forest. This walk includes an ascent of the gorgeous Whimble (which would make a lovely walk by itself).

Points of Interest:

1. Mutton Dingle. In an area of the world where so many sheep are to be found, the name Mutton Dingle must have a certain resonance for the human inhabitants of the environs (and, it must be supposed, a rather unpleasant one for the sheep), but as the easternmost of the three small valleys to the north west of New Radnor Mutton Dingle is the

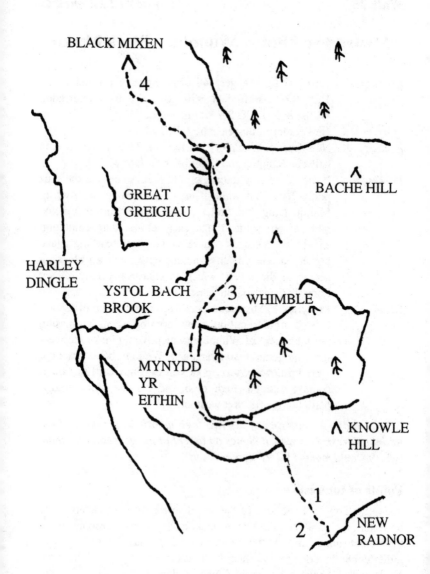

BLACK MIXEN

GREAT
GREIGIAU

BACHE HILL

HARLEY
DINGLE

YSTOL BACH
BROOK

WHIMBLE

MYNYDD
YR
EITHIN

KNOWLE
HILL

NEW
RADNOR

124

smallest and least impressive, though it is not without its charms. Unlike Harley Dingle to the south west of Black Mixen (see walk 14 for more information), it is at least possible to walk Mutton Dingle, though it is more pleasant to view it on the way to one of the area's higher points. Its western aspect, of course, is dominated by the rise to the Black Mixen plateau, but its eastern aspect is dominated by Knowle Hill, which is clearly visible from the metalled road up Mutton Dingle. Unfortunately Knowle Hill is largely enclosed, composed of farmland, but it is possible to circumnavigate the hill using public rights of way as shown on the 1:25 000 OS map.

2. New Radnor Castle. See walk 14.

3. Whimble. Although Whimble fails, by a matter of centimetres, to rise to 600m above sea level, it remains one of my favourite hills in Central Wales. It is a dramatic structure best viewed from a distance (it can best be seen in all its glory on the ascent to Great Rhos in walk 14), though even close up it seems to throw out a challenge to the walker to climb to the top. Its majestic conical shape inevitably draws comparisons with a number of other hills in Wales and the south west of England, notably the two Sugar Loaf mountains of Llanwrtyd Wells and the Black Mountains, Brent Tor on the western edge of Dartmoor and Glastonbury Tor in Somerset. Yet like all these hills, Whimble appears utterly dramatic from one side, but much gentler from the other. From the west Whimble appears almost impossibly steep, yet from the north (as you will see later in this walk) Whimble appears as a gentle dome. Certainly, the view from the summit is spectacular, and is my favourite viewpoint in the Radnor Forest. To the north east, Bache Hill rises majestically with its trig point clearly visible, and when the weather conditions are right you may see para-scenders engaged in their sport, parachutes billowing colourfully in the wind. To the north west, the mast atop Black Mixen stands starkly on the skyline, and in the valley it is easy to see the path of the bridleway that will take you there. To the west, of course, there is the summit plateau of Great Rhos - bleak and moody even in the best weather. Except in mist, it should be easy to spot at least one of the danger signs on the plateau, and it has to be said that you get a much better sense of Great Rhos as a mountain from this viewpoint than from Great Rhos itself.

Meanwhile to the east is the flatter land of the border plains - the contrast of hilly Wales and flatter England being quite striking.

4. Black Mixen. Like the plateau of Great Rhos across Harley Dingle to the west, the summit of Black Mixen does not present an impressive top, and it can be distinctly boggy underfoot, particularly after a spell of wet weather. However, for my taste, Black Mixen has a certain character that Great Rhos rather lacks, and this is perhaps a consequence of the transmitter mast at the top. To many walkers, it has to be admitted, the placing of masts atop some of our beautiful high places is little short of a crime against humanity, an act of despoilment to be condemned out of hand. To some walkers, though - and I must count myself among them - the occasional mast atop a summit is not so much of a problem. Indeed, where visibility is less than perfect, a looming mast can be a useful navigational aid. In the case of the mast upon Black Mixen, I think it adds to, rather than subtracts from, the interest of the summit, for here there is a unique - or at least highly unusual - juxtaposition of man-made structures. One the one hand there is a mast, a symbol of the most powerful medium of modern times and of the global transmission of information and education. On the other, though, there is a Bronze Age tumulus, a burial place of a millennia-old man or woman for whom something as commonplace to us as telecommunications would seem to be nothing less than pure magic. And to add the icing on the cake there is a dear old trig point, as modern as the science of precision surveying, yet in these days of GPS satellite systems as outdated and useless as the Bronze Age tumulus. What finer symbolism could there be of thousands of years of history, where progress has been the driving force of the achievements of the human race, yet where even the outdated is a potent reminder of our past? Will we, I wonder, in years to come be as tolerant of masts on out landscape as we are of tumuli and trig points? I rather doubt it! Although the summit of Black Mixen may have more interest than that of Great Rhos, it shares with it the curious feeling that the views on the way up are better than the views from the summit. Whimble, for example, is now out of sight, and only the very summit of Bache Hill is presented to the east. However, further to the south east it is now possible to make out the flat plains of the marches, and you may just

about be able to see the peaks of the Brecon Beacons away to the south. It is easy to convince yourself that you can detect the characteristic summit platforms of Corn Du and Pen y Fan, but it is more difficult to convince yourself that you are right!

Walk Directions:

1. The walk begins in the middle of New Radnor. Just north east of the main junction in the centre of the village (near the Post Office), a narrow metalled road (Mutton Dingle) heads up just west of north. This is probably the least attractive part of the walk and is certainly the hardest - a long uphill grind - but at least as you ascend the west side of Mutton Dingle [1] you can enjoy some great views of Knowle Hill to the east. Follow this road up past the remains of the old motte and bailey castle [2], past waymarked bridleways right and then left, and on to the end of the metalled section of the road at the edge of the forest. Here there is a fork: the right-hand fork leads into the forest, but we want the left-hand fork (signposted as a bridleway) which continues uphill roughly west, following the edge of the forest.

2. Follow the track west along the edge of the forestry, crossing a stile next to a metal gate, and keeping the wire fence at the edge of the forestry to your immediate right. It quickly swings north, still following the edge of the forestry, and still fairly steep, although you can console yourself with the knowledge that this represents the last of the steep climbing (except for the ascent of Whimble itself) and with the great view of Fron Hill to the west. The path here is still very obvious, following a series of pylons which continue almost to the top of Black Mixen itself. The dramatic rock face of Great Greigiau now comes into view away to the west of north. It is also now possible to see the Three Riggles away to the west, three great scree slopes dropping down the eastern face of the Great Rhos plateau down into Harley Dingle. You are now near the top of Mynydd yr Eithin, although if you want to attain the indistinct summit, only a few metres higher, you will have to chance your legs across the sea of heather to your left (heather-hopping is always a bit of a dicey business, in my experience, and it is probably not worth the risk - great views of Harley Dingle can be gained from walk 14). Continue north along the

path to the north western corner of the forestry. Whimble is now extremely obvious to the right. The best way to ascend to the summit of Whimble [3] is to cross the metal gate in front of you, then follow the obvious path to the top.

3. From the summit of Whimble, the only good way down to rejoin this walk is to retrace your steps back to the gate near the corner of the forestry. On the OS map, it looks tempting to strike off north from the summit to rejoin the bridleway further up, but the northern aspect of Whimble is very steep and likely to be dangerous. Furthermore, the northern boundary of Whimble's perimeter is enclosed by a barbed-wire fence, and so even if you managed to descend Whimble's north side you would probably have to walk back to the gate to re-join the bridleway in any case. On rejoining the bridleway, head north east and then north to the corner of the larger area of forestry to the north of Bache Hill. After the exertions so far, it is a relief to find that this section is fairly flat. Ystol Bach Brook bubbles merrily along deep down in the valley to the left, while Bache Hill looms high to your right. Note that the ford marked on the 1:25 000 OS map is unlikely to be a problem: except in flood conditions this is usually dry.

4. Before reaching the corner of the forestry, the bridleway takes a sharp right turn (leaving, at last, the line of pylons which continue straight uphill beyond the wire fence) before veering off left to the north again to a metal gate. Pass through the gate, to a clearing. At this point the path can become a little indistinct in places, but you should be able to make out a rough path veering away to the west beyond the gate, and this soon becomes a clearer path running west uphill towards the summit of Black Mixen. Head west uphill along this path, which roughly follows the course of a wire fence, and which eventually swings to the north west and on to the summit plateau of Black Mixen. This path can also become indistinct in places, and can be quite boggy as it veers away from the wire fence and across the head of Cwm Sian. Nevertheless, it will take you virtually to the summit, and the mast soon comes into view. The summit itself [4] is marked by a trig point - and, of course, by the mast which by now cannot be missed except in the very worst weather imaginable.

5. The best route to return to New Radnor is essentially the same way

you came, except that the ascent of Whimble can be missed out. Return along the bridleway down to the corner of the large forestry area north of Bache Hill, then head south towards Whimble. Follow the bridleway around Whimble to the south west and along and round the forestry area to Mutton Dingle and the start point at New Radnor.

Facilities:

New Radnor is well supplied with facilities. The Radnor Arms and the Eagle Inn both offer accommodation, and there are a number of bed and breakfast places and caravan and camping sites in the area. There is no Tourist Information Centre at New Radnor, but there is one at Builth Wells about a dozen miles or so to the west.

Safety Notes:

Most of this walk follows well-defined bridleways, where navigation should be no problem. In fact, in all but blanket mist the mast atop Black Mixen should provide even the most uncertain navigator, on reaching the summit, with an unmistakable target! Fortunately, too, most of the pathways are so clear that it should be almost impossible to miss your way. If blanket mist should descend while you are in the vicinity of the summit of Black Mixen, head south east to hit the path parallel with the wire fence leading to the forestry north of Bache Hill. If you should find yourself stranded on Whimble, head downhill - very carefully - just south of west along the path that you used to climb up, and this will bring you back to the bridleway that will take you back to New Radnor.

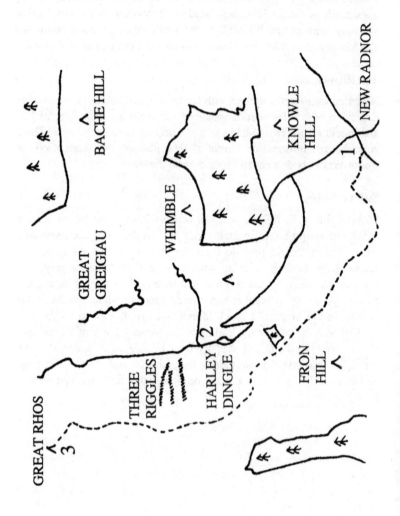

GREAT RHOS

THREE RIGGLES

HARLEY DINGLE

FRON HILL

GREAT GREIGIAU

WHIMBLE

BACHE HILL

KNOWLE HILL

NEW RADNOR

Fron Hill - Great Rhos

OS Maps:　　1:50 000 Landranger 148 (Presteigne & Hay-on-Wye); 1:25 000 Pathfinders 970 (SO 06/16: Llandrindod Wells) & 971 (SO 26/36: Presteigne).

Start:　　　Junction of the B4372 and the waymarked bridleway on the west side of New Radnor (GR 209 607).

Access:　　New Radnor is situated on the B4372 just off the A44 between Kington and Llanfihangel-Nant-Melan.

Parking:　　It should be easy to park on the street at or near the start point. Alternatively, there should be ample parking in New Radnor itself, from whence the start point will be only a few hundred metres walk at most.

Grade:　　Strenuous - involves about 420m of ascent. Walking boots essential - the bridleways soon take you out into wild mountain country and the high moorland can be quite boggy, particularly after wet weather.

A splendid walk out onto the second of the two high moorland plateaux of the Radnor Forest. Although the summit of Great Rhos itself is somewhat bleak, this is more than compensated for by the views down into the forbidden Harley Dingle from the ascent of Fron Hill.

Points of Interest:

1. New Radnor and New Radnor Castle. It is somewhat confusing that the old county of Radnorshire (now part of the county of Powys) contains two Radnors - Old Radnor (some three miles to the east) and New Radnor. In fact from the point of view of a visitor today, both Radnors are old, though as the name suggests Old Radnor is the older of the two. Indeed, there is evidence of human habitation at Old Radnor dating back to about 2000 BC, when the New Stone Age was giving way to the Bronze Age. New Radnor, on the other hand, is

thought to have grown up a mere one thousand or so years ago, primarily as a garrison town to service the castle that had been built at the site, and it soon supplanted Old Radnor as the primary settlement in the area. The first castle at New Radnor - which is marked "Motte and Bailey" on the 1:25 000 OS map - was built in 1064, and it was to undergo considerable change and to witness many crucial battles and other important political events over the next five or six centuries. The original wooden structure of 1064 was built by Harold, Earl of Hereford (later to become King of England and to gain fame as the loser of the Battle of Hastings). Harold was engaged in a titanic struggle for domination of the area with Gruffudd ap Llywelyn, King of Gwynedd and effective ruler of virtually the whole of Wales. Several years earlier, Gruffudd had destroyed Harold's original stronghold at Old Radnor, and had made an alliance with the northern Saxons of Mercia against the Western Saxons of Wessex, of whom Harold was a leading light. Now, however, Harold was making a comeback, and used his castle at New Radnor as a base to attack Gruffudd's stronghold at Rhuddlan. Harold was successful, and Gruffudd was killed, but just as it seemed Harold would overrun all of Wales his attention was diverted elsewhere - not least to Hastings, where the Normans were preparing his nemesis. Although at first this may have seemed a lucky escape for the Welsh, the Normans were to prove an even more formidable foe. New Radnor fell into the hands of the de Braose family, and a second more substantial motte and bailey castle was built on the castle site. The area remained under Norman domination until 1196, when Rhys ap Gruffudd re-captured it for the Welsh, but this interlude was brief, for following the death of Rhys in 1197 the locals were again ousted from power, and the de Braose family were back in residence the following year. Domination over the castle and its environment continued to be disputed for most of the next century, until finally, in 1233, it fell into the hands of the Mortimer family. Despite the odd hiccup, particularly during the time of Llywelyn ap Gruffudd towards the end of the thirteenth century, the castle remained in the hands of the Mortimers up to the time of Owain Glyndŵr, and indeed the Mortimers had it rebuilt in stone in 1275. After the defeat of Glyndŵr in the fifteenth century, the remains of the castle passed to the King, and it became a prison for a while. The life of New Radnor Castle was effectively at an end, although it did serve briefly to house a Royalist garrison during the English Civil War. Today, there is little left of New Radnor Castle, although the remnants of the earthworks may easily be visited by following the footpath past the church from the centre of town, or, more conveniently from the point of view of this walk, following the footpath from the western side where it meets the bridlepath at GR 209 609. New Radnor has other claims to fame besides the castle, of course. It was here, in the twelfth century, that Geraldus Cambrensis became the first Welshman to volunteer for the crusades, and New Radnor became an important centre for the development of the Baptist movement in Wales in the seventeenth century. However, although New Radnor was indeed the administrative centre of the county of Radnorshire from the Act of Union of 1536, its influence over the years waned in favour of the growing town of Presteigne, and after the English Civil War Presteigne became the county town (despite the fact that Presteigne had held out in the Royalist cause). Today, New Radnor remains a peaceful and pretty village, its colourful - and often violent - history very much behind it. The memorial, obvious as soon as you enter the village, is to commemorate a local figure, Sir George Cornewall Lewis, and it was designed by John Gibbs, who also designed the Shakespeare Memorial in Stratford-upon-Avon.

2. Harley Dingle. When one thinks of the valleys of Wales, one thinks of the industrialised south. However, there is more than one type of valley in Wales, and although the great scarred population centres of Glamorgan and Gwent may have captured the imagination of novelists and film makers, there are many smaller, and distinctly more picturesque, valleys all over the country. New Radnor hardly figures alongside Rhondda and Blaenau Gwent, perhaps, but there are valleys here all the same. They are small and they are beautiful, yet even here the valleys are not devoid of the scars of the march of technology that has been the hallmark of the twentieth century. To the north east of New Radnor lies a quaint sequence of three valleys - Davy Morgan's Dingle, Harley Dingle and Mutton Dingle - all of which possess a surfeit of natural beauty. What a shame it is, therefore, that the middle

valley, the larger of the three, should be out of bounds to the walker. For this valley, Harley Dingle, has been in use since the 1930s as a testing range for munitions, and there is a multitude of danger signs all around the valley, covering every possible access point, warning the walker that entry into it is absolutely, definitely, forbidden. We can only feel frustrated, then, as we climb up Fron Hill, by the wonderful walk that Harley Dingle would provide if only it could, with Great Rhos dominating on one side and Black Mixen dominating on the other. To compound the frustration, I have never seen or heard munitions testing here, and I have never talked to another walker who has. Yet until the authorities decide otherwise, one of the great valley walks of Central Wales is denied to us.

3. Great Rhos. It is a most peculiar mountain, Great Rhos. It would be nice to think that the wonderful valley views you can enjoy on the way up would be rounded off by even more wonderful mountaintop views from the summit. After all, at 660m above sea level it is the highest point among the mountains of the Radnor Forest. Yet somehow Great Rhos doesn't feel like a great mountain at all. It is some ten metres taller than its perennial neighbour Black Mixen, but it doesn't seem to have the character than Black Mixen can offer, and it always seems to me that the views on the way up to the summit are rather better than the views from the summit itself - it is certainly true that the going underfoot is much worse as you approach the summit than it is on the slopes you have climbed to get there. How can this be so? The problem of Great Rhos is that it doesn't really feel like a summit. It *is* a summit, of course - the climb up to it can leave you in no doubt of that - but as a glance at the map will demonstrate its top consists of a wide, flat plateau nearly a whole kilometre in length and about half a kilometre in width, so the walker is denied that unique feeling of exposed height so characteristic of many of Wales' peaks. In truth, this is, like much of the Cwmdeuddwr area, really an area of high moorland of the type that will be familiar to any walker of an area such as Dartmoor. Except following a prolonged period of hot and dry weather, the top of Great Rhos is very boggy, and the terrain is oddly featureless. Indeed, one is quite grateful for the trig point, for otherwise it would be nearly impossible to decide where the true

summit is. Even the view from the trig is strangely unsatisfying. The relentlessly rolling hills in all directions that are such a hallmark of hill walking in Central Wales seem distant and disconnected, and the dramatic dome of Whimble is now out of sight. Indeed the view is dominated solely by the plateau to the east of Black Mixen. For some odd reason, it always seems to me that Black Mixen, with its ancient Bronze Age tumuli and its rakish, modern transmitter mast, is having so much more fun than Great Rhos, and would not swap its history-spanning accoutrements for Great Rhos' extra ten metres of height for all the tea in China! Still, it should not be thought that Great Rhos is without its charms, even if they are eccentric charms. For if one word can be used to sum up Great Rhos, then that word is *bleak*. There is nothing ostentatious here - no breath-taking panorama, no craggy splendour, no majestic peak. There is simply a boggy plateau that, except in the very best of summer weather, is damp, cold and windswept. Realism, rather than romance, rules the roost here. If you like your open countryside bleak, you will love Great Rhos. Me? I prefer Black Mixen.....

Walk Directions:

1. The walk begins where the waymarked bridleway (Newgate Lane) on the west side of New Radnor meets the B4372 (GR 209 607). Follow the bridleway north westish, passing the entrance to the footpath leading east to the castle [1] and the church, until the bridleway veers left and starts to climb uphill. The way remains very clear, and you pass through a metal gate, before the path starts to cross more or less open fields. However, the bridlepath is still clear as it contours round the steep hill to Harley Dingle.

2. As the clear path veers round to the right, heading north west, you start to descend to the substantial stream formed by the confluence of Ystol Bach Brook and the brook leading from Shepherd's Well away to the north. Pass through the blue gate, and down to the junction with the other bridleway leading up from Highgate Farm on the main road. Turn right here, and you are confronted with the first warning sign informing you that you are not allowed into Harley Dingle. Follow the waymarked bridleway to the left and through the gate down to the

stream. There was, at one point, a ford here, but the stream now really deserves to be called a river, and it would be foolhardy (and very wet!) to attempt to ford the stream. Fortunately, however, a wooden bridge has been erected over the stream, allowing us to keep our feet dry. Cross the bridge and continue along the waymarked bridleway uphill to the north west.

3. Continue up the very obvious bridleway leading up the eastern slope of Fron Hill. There is a stiff climb of about a kilometre or so ahead. Fortunately, though, the superb views along and across Harley Dingle [2] give us ample reasons (or excuses!) to stop to catch our breath on the way up. The dingle itself, unfortunately, is out of bounds to us, but the hills to the east of the dingle become ever more spectacular the further up Fron Hill we travel. As you pass the small area of forestry to the west of Upper Harley, the mast atop Black Mixen comes into view, and to the south and south east of this the characteristic outlines of Mynydd yr Eithin and Whimble are unmistakable. Whimble, in particular, is striking. Like Glastonbury Tor in Somerset and the Sugar Loaf near Llanwrtyd Wells, Whimble looks almost impossible to climb from this angle, yet the steepness is deceptive. Steep it may be, but it is perfectly walkable (and it is visited in walk 13). Bache Hill, to the east of Black Mixen, may also be visible, and its unnamed foothill (the spot height of 604m at GR 208 632) certainly becomes visible as you ascend Fron Hill, its Bronze Age tumuli quite clear in decent weather.

4. Eventually, the bridleway bends round to the left as it approaches the disused quarry (at GR 188 621), and it follows its way past a danger sign and around the quarry workings bending once again to the right towards north west. Pass through the gate here, and follow the waymarked path uphill. After a couple of hundred metres or so, you will arrive at a fork in the way marked by an upright wooden post bearing a waymark. The left hand fork follows the path of the main bridleway marked on the map, heading off north west into Davy Morgan's Dingle. However, it is the right hand fork that we want, and this heads off just west of north uphill towards the summit plateau of Great Rhos. This path continues fairly obviously but still fairly steeply, until (at long last!) the terrain starts to flatten out a bit round about the

600m contour line. By now the views along Davy Morgan's Dingle to the west are quite spectacular, and Whimble is still dramatic away to the east, though the mast on Black Mixen is now popping in and out of view. The bridleway is still fairly easy to follow, more or less due north, and another danger sign alongside the path marks our way ahead quite nicely.

5. Passing the danger sign, continue to follow the bridleway due north. Unfortunately, the path soon starts to become less distinct and much boggier, and our task is rather complicated by the profusion of paths that seem to criss-cross the summit plateau of Great Rhos. This is definitely a case where the compass is the best guide - keep to the best path available heading more or less due north. A little less than a kilometre due north of the last danger sign there is a wire fence and another danger sign (at GR 185 637). There is also a gate here - pass through the gate.

6. Continue forward about 25m or so on the other side of the gate, to a fairly distinct path off to the left, roughly parallel with the fence. Turn left and follow this path. Very soon the trig point will come into view on the right. It is possible to strike off directly for the trig here, but it is very difficult going over the heather. It is much easier to continue along this path until the trig is due north, at which point a path leading directly to the trig should come into view. Now you can simply follow this path to the trig at the summit of Great Rhos [3].

7. The tussocky going around the summit plateau of Great Rhos makes the route we have come up easily the best route to go down again. After enjoying the bleak vastness of the Great Rhos highland, the way to go is simply to re-trace your steps back to the gate in the wire fence. Then follow the best tracks more or less due south back to the main bridlepath near to the disused quarry to the east of Davy Morgan's Dingle (at GR 188 621), and then follow the obvious bridleways back to the start point at New Radnor.

Facilities:

As described in walk 13, New Radnor is well supplied with facilities. The Radnor Arms and the Eagle Inn both offer accommodation, and there are a number of bed and breakfast places and caravan and camping sites in the area. There is no Tourist Information Centre at New Radnor, but there is one at Builth Wells about a dozen miles or so to the west.

Safety Notes:

Most of this walk follows well-defined bridleways, where navigation should be no problem. About the only place where navigation in mist might be a little difficult is on the high moorland of Great Rhos itself, where the bridleways can become a little indistinct in places. If stranded at the summit trig, bear south until you reach the wire fence, then turn left to follow the fence roughly north east until you reach the bridlepath at the gate (GR 185 637). Then follow the best available paths due south until you hit the main bridlepath (GR 186 621) running south east down Fron Hill towards the start point. If stranded anywhere south of the wire fence on the high moorland of Great Rhos, the best plan is to bear due south. Sooner or later you must hit the main north west-south east bridlepath leading from Davy Morgan's Dingle to Fron Hill. The main danger here, however, is that you may encounter ground falling away very steeply south west into Davy Morgan's Dingle itself. If this happens, change direction to the south east, when you must hit either the main north west-south east bridlepath or (more likely) the bridlepath leading south from the wire fence near the summit. In any case, follow the path roughly south/south east back over Fron Hill to the start point. In any event, it is important to avoid the temptation to head due east down into Harley Dingle. This will not only take you down into the danger area, but will also take you down some dangerously steep ground.

Selected Bibliography

Batt, T. (1994): *Place-names in the 3000 ft Mountains of Wales*.
   Llanrwst: Gwasg Carreg Gwalch.

Burnham, H. (1995): *A Guide to Ancient and Historic Wales: Clwyd
   and Powys*. London: HMSO.

Davies, J. C. (1911): *Folk-lore of West and Central Wales*. Lampeter:
   Llanerch (Facsimile reprint 1992).

Gregory, D. (1989): *Wales Before 1066: A Guide*. Llanrwst: Gwasg
   Carreg Gwalch.

Gregory, D. (1993): *Wales Before 1536: A Guide*. Llanrwst: Gwasg
   Carreg Gwalch.

Gregory, D. (1995): *Wales After 1536: A Guide*. Llanrwst: Gwasg
   Carreg Gwalch.

Houlder, C. (1978): *Wales: An Archeological Guide*. London: Faber
   and Faber.

Jones, G. and Jones, T. (Transl: 1974): *The Mabinogion*. London:
   Dent.

Morris, J. (1984): *The Matter of Wales*. London: Penguin.

Prager, C. (1998): *The Rambler's Yearbook and Accommodation
   Guide 1998*. London: Rambler's Association.

Rees, S. (1992): *A Guide to Ancient and Historic Wales: Dyfed*.
   London: HMSO.

Sale, R. (1984): *The Wye Valley*. Hounslow: Wildwood House.

Williams, G. A. (1985): *When Was Wales?* London: Penguin.